GW01311236

BUSINESS
IMPROVEMENT QUICK

Understand, Identify, Improve.

JOSEPH MANN MSc

Published by Joseph Mann

© 2023 Derby
First published by Joseph Mann in 2023, Derby
ISBN: 9798373776097
www.businessimprovementquick.com

Disclaimer:

All rights reserved. No part of this book may be reproduced or modified in any form, including photocopying, recording, or by any information storage and retrieval system, without permission in writing from the publisher.

This book is designed to provide information and motivation to learners of Business Improvement. Any information in this book is strictly for educational purposes. If you wish to apply ideas contained in this book then you are taking full responsibility for your own actions.

Business Improvement Quick

Understand, Identify, Improve.

Joseph Mann MSc

Table of Contents

List of Tables and Figures

Introduction

Business improvement is an increasingly important topic for many organisations. A good company makes continual changes to improve the way in which they work – this is also known as "Continuous Improvement". The best companies strive consistently for perfection.

To change a company for the better you need to do two things
1. Identify problems to work on (What I call **Understand** and **Identify**)
2. Solve the problems and implement permanent fixes (What I call **Improve**)

Companies are often good at one of these two things, but rarely both. To be among the best companies in the world, both of these areas need to be mastered.

What's true for companies is also true for employees and careers. Business leaders of tomorrow can make a name for themselves today by applying and using the tools and techniques given in this book. Done properly, business improvement directly impacts the bottom line – *the* key measure of business success.

Lean and Six Sigma are methodologies that can enable companies to achieve this. Think of these, and the other methods and topics covered in this book as tools. It's not just having the right tools, but being able to utilise them properly and effectively.

The business improvement library normally covers two categories; academic textbooks on detailed theory, or "how to" guides that already assume a high level of current knowledge. This book provides the middle ground; whether you're new to the topic or already an expert, the theory and the tools are explained in an easy-to-understand way, that you can quickly and simply apply. After reading you'll be able to put the tools into practise and understand how businesses should operate.

There are three main sections in the book. In the first section, titled "Business Improvement Primer" (page 18), I'll focus on the theory of business improvement and explain all the key concepts. Next, in "Improvement Tools and Techniques" I've included all the tools and techniques that I've found most useful in my career. You'll understand how to put these into practise with various real-world examples included throughout. Finally, I've included a section on "Project Management" (page 128). Project management and business improvement are inextricably linked, with skills in both required to be a good business improver.

Key templates used during the various sections are in the appendices (from page 152). These templates are also found on the website (www.BusinessImprovementQuick.com).

There's also an index section (page 165). at the end of the book and I recommend you go here if there's a specific area you want to understand more. I've tried to follow a logical order as much as possible throughout the book, particularly where the tools and techniques are concerned, by presenting them in an order in which they might be utilised in real-world scenarios.

So, when you're ready, let's begin. Happy improving!

Business Improvement Primer

In this chapter we'll consider the basics of theory of Business improvement; focusing on the topics of Lean and Six Sigma (and Lean Six Sigma!). Following this I'll introduce some improvement methodologies before sharing my own approach to improvement; the Understand, Identify, Improve method.

What is Lean?

The exact answer to the question posed above has eluded top academics for many years. It seems it's only possible to agree on a theme of Lean so long as you are not precise about it. Of course the word Lean itself, as an adjective, means someone (or something) that is both thin and healthy. In a simple way, I like to think of a Lean business being a thin and healthy one. In its essence, Lean is all about doing more with less resources. Lean is most often associated with the car manufacturer Toyota.

Whilst appropriately defining Lean is something that has been debated for a long time, I found through my previous research that it almost always comes down to the following five points:

1. **Focusing on customer requirements** - thinking about who the customers are and what, exactly, they want from your products. Everything should then work towards delivering that.
2. **A relationship with organisational culture** - the way people work in the company needs to have Lean in mind. The "culture" of the organisation should support Lean and business improvement. Culture is the thoughts and way that a group of people act – so organisational culture means this for an organisation – the ideas and behaviour of an organisation. The best companies have a Lean (organisational) culture.
3. **Focusing on increasing quality** - high quality (within the customers' requirements) should be something everyone in the company aims for. Quality refers to how good something is in relation to a set standard (perhaps measuring a product against customer requirements).

4. **A pursuit of perfection** - the whole company and all of its employees should have a goal of perfection (of being the "ideal company").
5. **Focusing on reducing waste** - anything that isn't adding value is waste. Everyone should be focused on removing this (see the below section on waste for more information).

These five factors come together as self-supporting elements of Lean within an organisation:

The Self-Supporting Elements of Lean

So, to be Lean, a company will produce what the customer wants, to the highest quality, at the lowest cost, in the shortest time and with maximum flexibility. Often, though, the perfect world isn't immediately possible; there are trade-offs required in quality, cost or delivery. I remember seeing something like the following on a poster in an office:

- You can have a high-quality product that's cheap but you'll have to wait
- You can have a high-quality product delivered quickly but it will be expensive
- You can have a cheap product delivered quickly but it will be poor quality

We'll come back to the themes of quality, cost and delivery later (See page 65).

Six Sigma (6σ)

Briefly, it's worth turning our attention to Six Sigma, another often discussed improvement methodology. Whilst Lean might be associated with Toyota, Six Sigma has links with another organisation; Motorola. To understand what Six Sigma is, we first need to understand what "sigma" is. Sigma is a letter from the Greek alphabet ("σ"). It represents a statistical value with the sixth level resulting in fewer than "3.4 defects per million opportunities". This means that it is essentially a quality target for processes and businesses to aim for. The "sigma level" that a process achieves can be used to define the level of variation being seen.

Consider the following process output. Imagine a process that cuts a metal block – removing a rough edge of excess material. The width of this block is measured afterwards – it should be exactly 10mm (but we allow a tolerance of plus or minus ($\pm$) 1mm – more on this later!).

Process Output Histogram Example

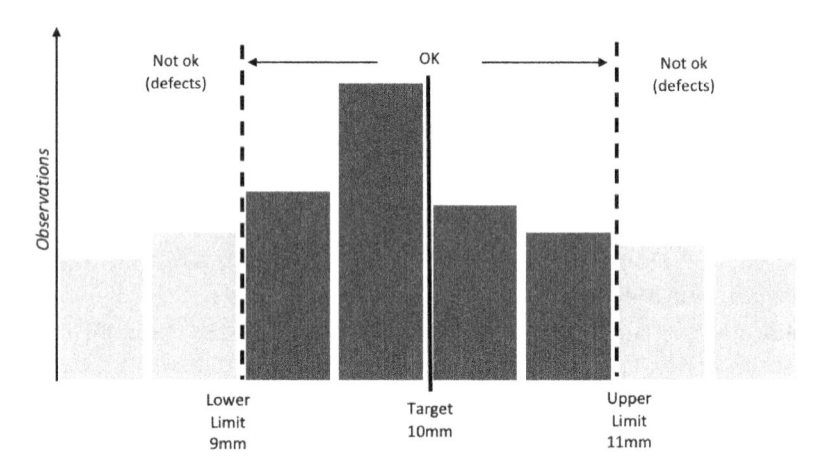

The output products of this process have been measured to understand if we are meeting what the customer wants. Basically, the customer wants what is inside the dotted line (labelled "ok"), the process is also producing outside of that remit (out of tolerance – "not ok"). Failing (even sometimes) to meet the customer requirements demonstrates that there are some problems that need resolving. It also means that there's scope to make improvements and save money!

Remember that Six Sigma aims to have fewer than 3.4 Defects Per Million Opportunities (DPMO), but there are different levels of Sigma, summarised in the table below (if you're interested, the process above has a sigma level of approximately 2 Sigma).

Sigma Levels Table

Sigma Level	DPMO	% Right
1	691,462	30.85380%
2	308,538	69.14620%
3	66,807	93.31930%
4	6,210	99.37900%
5	233	99.97670%
6	3.4	99.99966%
7	0.019	100.00000%

In some industries it is much more vital to operate at a higher Sigma level. Remember also that this concept doesn't just apply to manufacturing processes (the same goes for the majority of Lean or improvement concepts too). Another benchmark often used in some industries is 3.8 Sigma (which equates to 99% right). Here's a few examples to compare 6 Sigma to 3.8 Sigma:

- The United States Postal Service handles approximately 425 million items of mail each day – if they operate at 6 Sigma level then they will lose 1445 mail items per day, at 3.8 Sigma it's 4.25 million per day!
- The UK National Health Service (NHS) issues approximately 1 billion medical prescriptions per year. At 6 Sigma that's 3400 incorrect prescriptions per year, whilst at 3.8 Sigma it's 10 million.

Lean Six Sigma

The statistical understanding of processes given by Six Sigma, alongside the relentless focus on customer requirements and waste drive through Lean have meant that, understandably, companies want to get the best of both worlds. This has led to the creation of a joined-up approach; Lean Six Sigma. A lot of companies are now training their employees in these tools and techniques. A generally accepted tiered training system involves the award of *belts*. The training required looks something like the summary below (but training and terminology may differ from company to company – for example, I know of one company who referred to Lean as "process excellence" just to ensure they sounded different to the competition!)

Lean Six Sigma Belts Training Summary Table

White Belt / Yellow Belt	1 day training course ("awareness of improvement")
Green Belt	1 – 2-week training course, 3–6-month improvement project ("practitioner of improvement")
Black Belt	Above plus 2 – 4-week training course (or longer), 1-year, complex improvement project ("leader in improvement")
Master Black Belt	Above plus another Black Belt style project ("expert in improvement")

Summary of Methodologies

To summarise, Lean and Six Sigma (and Lean Six Sigma) provide companies with methodologies to improve themselves. Remember that to change a company for the better you can't just do the improving – you've got to understand the wider company first – know where the gaps are. Then you can identify your priorities for improvement before actually enacting the improvements themselves.

If it sounds easy – it isn't. One thing that often stands in the way here is culture. Specifically, organisational culture. Culture is one of those difficult to define concepts that every group of people (including in individual businesses) has. Culture can act either as a sort of runway for ideas and improvements to take off on… or it can act as a deadweight, holding an organisation back. Companies need to be wary of this and ensure they bring employees with them on an improvement journey. Take it one step at a time and ensure everyone is involved (and engaged) who needs to be.

From what we've considered so far, we can create a (very) rough improvement equation; this is what companies need in order to become what we term a *Lean Enterprise* – a successful, Lean organisation.

An Organisational Improvement Equation

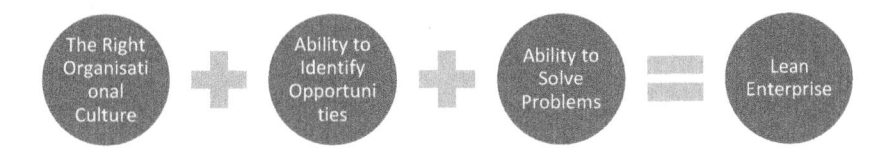

A Lean enterprise is a company that properly applies all the Lean principles – it's what every organisation should strive to become. Very few organisations can claim to be a Lean enterprise – perhaps Toyota is the best example.

With the above in mind, and with years of experience managing projects and improving businesses, my method for improving businesses is to follow three key steps:

1. Understand
2. Identify
3. Improve

As you'll see, this method is reliant on using various tools and techniques that I will introduce throughout this book. There are many improvement methodologies – and I'm not precious about everyone following only the above – be flexible and choose whatever comes most naturally to you.

The table below shows my three stages (Understand, Identify, Improve) alongside a very common Lean methodology (Plan, Do, Check, Act: PDCA) and a Six Sigma methodology (DMAIC):

Methodology Comparison Table

Understand		
Identify	Plan	Define
		Measure
		Analyse
Improve	Do	Improve
	Check	Control
	Act	

The PDCA and DMAIC methodologies don't fully cover the first point here: the *understanding*. They are principally focused on either solving a specific problem (DMAIC) or on *planning* (PDCA). Planning should be the biggest area in any problem solving activity (this is partly why Plan covers three elements of DMAIC; Define, Measure and Analyse), but before that a would-be business improver first needs to *understand* the wider business. Understanding the business enables problems to be identified more easily, prioritised and then solved. We can quickly summarise the above one more time as follows:

1. Understand the business/environment
2. Identify the problems
3. Solve the problems

Now we'll briefly go through the DMAIC and PDCA processes, alongside some core improvement terminology and principles, then we'll get straight into how to employ the Understand, Identify, Improve methodology appropriately using the tools and techniques within this book.

Plan Do Check Act (PDCA)

PDCA stands for Plan, Do, Check, Act and is also known as the "Deming Cycle" – having been invented by Dr William Edwards Deming. Here's how we might define each stage:

- Plan – Identify an improvement and assess it
- Do – Implement as planned
- Check – How did the improvement perform versus the plan?
- Act – Complete any further actions as required.

PDCA is a continuous cycle of improvement, and is often shown as the following diagram:

The PDCA Cycle

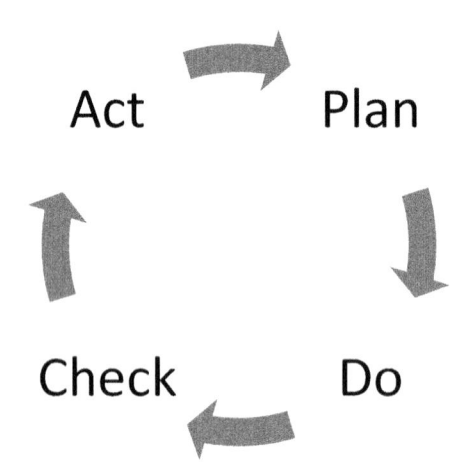

Furthermore, the cycle can be shown as part of an organisations efforts to improve over time:

The PDCA Cycle Over Time

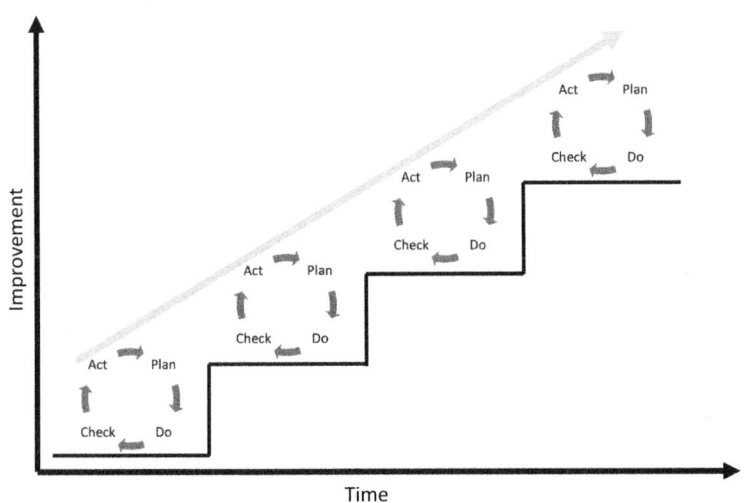

If you zoom out and take a look holistically at an entire organisation (one that is adopting and using Lean principles of course) you will see the continued use of the cycle to better the organisation. Each step in this diagram represents *standardisation* (standardisation is covered in more depth in the next section. See page 35). You can only properly improve if you have a clear, consistent baseline to improve *from*. To move to the next level, we plan for what that might look like (Plan), enact it cautiously (Do) and then test to ensure it's working appropriately (Check and Act). This process is repeated numerous times, in order to repeatedly take the business forward. This is the definition of Continuous Improvement (CI) – sometimes referred to as Kaizen.

The PDCA cycle is particularly important as it was one of the first problem solving methods to be created. As such, almost all business improvement methodologies follow the same logical structure, as we saw in the table in the previous section.

Define, Measure, Analyse, Improve, Control (DMAIC)

While the PDCA cycle is generally associated more with Lean, the DMAIC cycle is a Six Sigma creation. DMAIC is a five-step problem solving process, I'll outline each of the stages below:

1. D – Define
2. M – Measure
3. A – Analyse
4. I – Improve
5. C – Control

In the Define stage, you firstly *define* exactly what the problem is that needs solving. SMART objectives, a problem and a goal statement are absolutely key here (see page 90). Often in this phase, we will want to prove that the problem is relevant to the customer and that it will provide clear, justifiable business benefits.

With Measure, we want to understand what we call the current state – how is the process we're looking to improve performing right now. We need to get as much data as possible to understand whether the process is performing how we expect it to. Within this stage we would expect to include a process map (see page 48). It might include run charts (page 68) and the use of KPIs (page 61).

Analyse – Next, we can brainstorm hypotheses (i.e. potential root causes) for the problem(s). This stage is then all about 'testing the hypotheses' using statistics (see page 119). In this stage, using the data we have available, we will look into the potential reasons and prove the ultimate root cause of the problem(s). We may use techniques like an FMEA (see page

86) an Ishikawa diagram (see page 95) and the five whys (see page 98).

When we reach the Improve phase, we now know what the root cause of our problem is. Next, we need to take action to improve it. In this stage we will create, choose and then implement the best solutions to our problem. This needs to be done in a controlled way and with as much care as possible. Techniques like SCAMPER (see page 100) and brainstorming (page 93) can help us to achieve this.

The Control phase is all about ensuring any solution you have put in place is permanent. We want to make sure that the solution has been embedded and that the problem is now removed. People sometimes use the phrase "make sure it's not just a sticking plaster!" which is where a solution has not fully solved the root case of a problem, but might appear as though it has done – this scenario must be avoided. Once we are sure we have solved the problem properly, we can finish the project. Perhaps we will implement new KPIs (page 61), error proofing (page 111) or a run chart (page 68) to monitor and control the process performance in the future.

The Customer, Process Improvement, Standardisation and Tolerances

Four key terms that I want to make sure we understand before we move on are:
- The Customer
- Process Improvement
- Standardisation
- Tolerances

Improvement means that we must think about the customer a little more loosely than we might do in general business management. The customer is in relation to the thing we are trying to improve. If it's the whole business we're improving, then yes, the customer is the person/company that we sell products to. If we're looking at one small process – who does that process deliver to? Perhaps we're improving a goods in area of a company – in this case our customer might be the manufacturing process. Lean Improvement is first and foremost about delivering what the customer wants – so we need to ensure we're considering the right one!

Process improvement is fairly self-explanatory, but remember that the process we're improving doesn't just have to be a manufacturing process – it can be an office-based process (often termed a *transactional* process). It could be the whole process within purchasing, one small part of a machining process or the logistics process for delivery from the supply chain. Anything that can be defined in stages (or steps) – with a defined beginning and end – is a process. If it's a process then we can map it (we'll come on to process mapping later), standardise it and improve it.

Which brings us onto (once again) standardisation. Standardisation is the bedrock of improvement. If everyone isn't working to a standard then the customer isn't getting the same output every time (whether we're talking here about an internal or external customer). Sometimes the output might be better than expected, other times worse than expected – but because it isn't standardised it is not meeting the customer's expectations each and every time. If we're thinking Lean – that's a problem!

So companies need to speak to their customers and understand clear boundaries and expectations. These will be against various different measures or variables. These are known as tolerances. For example, most products produced in a factory will have dimensional tolerances: by this we mean an upper or lower limit (measurement) perhaps in length, width and depth. Remember our process from earlier where we're cutting a metal block? The width of this block is measured afterwards and should be exactly 10mm, we call this the "nominal" – this is the target width. We have an upper or lower limit of 11mm and 9mm respectively. So the width of this block, a requirement that should be defined by the customer, is 10mm ± 1mm. We can draw the nominal and our tolerance limits on a chart like this:

Run Chart of Block Width Over Time

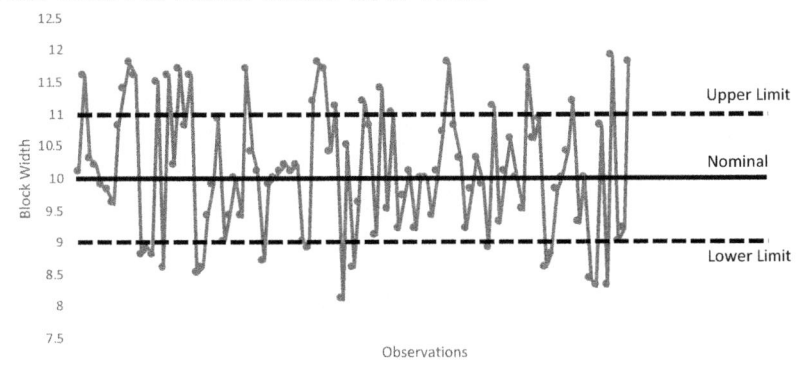

This chart is a run chart of our process data (sometimes also called a time series plot or a control chart – particularly if we're using it to validate an improvement). You can compare this with the histogram we saw in the Six Sigma section earlier (page 24) as another way to show process data – although this time we also have a time element to compare with. Once again, this chart allows us to see that the process is regularly producing out of tolerance – an improvement is required.

Once tolerances are set, processes need to be standardised too. We can ask ourselves; what is the best way of doing a particular process to produce the output that matches what the customer wants? Initially some experimentation may be needed but once a process is decided upon it should be documented and rigidly adhered to. Remember that just because a process is documented doesn't mean that everyone is doing what it says – this should be checked regularly and action taken to ensure we are achieving standardisation (going back to our PDCA cycle discussed earlier!).

If every process and product in a company is standardised, we're able to properly apply the principles of continuous improvement. This is because, fundamentally, you can't improve something if you don't know where you're starting from. You need to know the current state in order to build on it.

Understand, Identify, Improve

Now we've covered much of the basics of Lean improvement, let's introduce the Understand, Identify, Improve methodology to bring it all together. Something that this method does differently (to DMAIC or PDCA) is to shift (initially) the focus onto the business as a whole, rather than on the resolution of individual problems (as such, I might decide to use my methodology for a whole business but could then choose to use a 7-Step (page 102) or DMAIC process to solve a specific problem – particularly when we get to the Improve stage).

Businesses might choose to go through the full Understand, Identify, Improve cycle each year. Firstly **understanding** the business and areas of opportunity, then **identifying** specific cost savings and finally enacting those **improvement** projects. The outcomes will be a list of problems and opportunities to improve the company and save money:

Understand, Identify, Improve Flow Chart

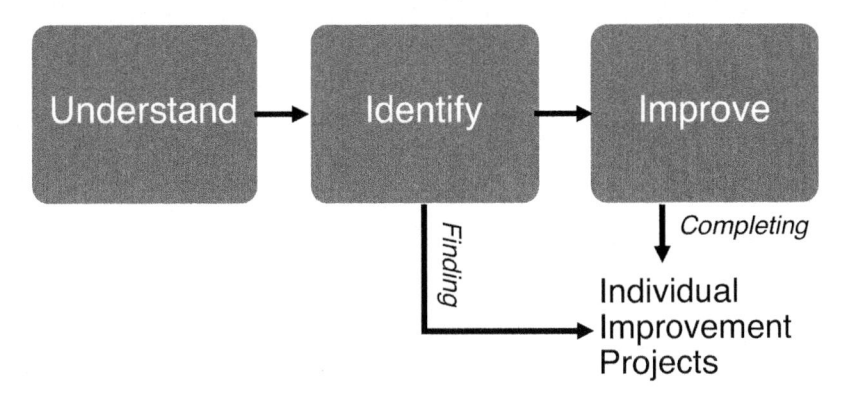

The process can be summarised further with the following table:

Understand, Identify, Improve Summary Table

Stage	Input	Key Question	Example Tools	Output
Understand	Stakeholders, business knowledge, desire to improve	Where do we need to focus?	TIMWOOD, Process Mapping, Go-Look-See	Areas of opportunity. "Gaps"
Identify	Areas of Opportunity. "Gaps"	What's causing us the most pain?	Pareto, "Cost Out Workshops", Ease / Effect Matrix	Prioritised Problems and Projects
Improve	Prioritised Problems and Projects	How can we solve these problems?	7-Step, DMAIC, SCAMPER, Ishikawa	Completed Projects, Cost Savings, New Standards.

Understand

The understand phase gives a clear direction and place to begin with the improvement journey. It's about gathering data to understand the here and now, the "current state" of an organisation. Only once we've mapped key processes, seen them in action and really *understood* the business, can we build upon that to improve it. This stage sets the foundation for improvement by giving an understanding of the main areas of waste and areas of potential opportunity. For Understand, some key areas to understand include Waste (page 42), Process Mapping (page 48) and Go-Look-See (page 46).

Identify

Taking the broad areas of opportunity, it's now time to identify specific problems within them. The Pareto principle, in particular, comes in handy here (see page 77). We'll look at the gaps and understand where, specifically, we need to focus on to make a material difference to the organisation. The outputs from this stage are a list of opportunities – often we'll prioritise these using an ease / effect matrix (page 83).

Improve

Now we have a thorough understanding of the business and have identified the specific problems we want to tackle. So it's all about improving them – solving the key problems one by one to result in a better, "leaner" organisation. The key technique used here is the 7-Step approach to problem solving (see page 102).

<u>Improvement Tools and Techniques</u>

<u>Waste and TIMWOOD</u>

What is a problem? What needs resolving? In almost all cases, it's waste. Waste is something a company does or makes that does not provide value to the customer. Waste costs a company to product, but cannot bring any value at all back in. The TIMWOOD model, developed from the original wastes identified by Toyota's Taiichi Ohno, helps with the identification of waste by putting them into categories:

- **T - Transportation**
- **I - Inventory**
- **M - Movement**
- **W - Wait-time**
- **O - Overproduction**
- **O - Over-processing**
- **D - Defects**

Below are some examples of what might be considered waste in each category:

Transportation - a lorry moving a part from one factory to another. A ship carrying material around the world. Could all this be done in one factory or one location?

Inventory - lots of products stored on a shelf. If customers aren't buying products, they can become obsolete. Think about inventory as a business's money sat [stuck] on a shelf, which cannot be accessed.

Movement - an operator (or a "machinist") needing to walk 10 metres every 10 minutes to pick up a particular tool. An office worker walking 50 metres to get to a printer or computer.

Wait-time - anything that is sat idle [motionless] waiting for something. A person needing to wait for instructions or for someone else to finish their part of a task.

Overproduction – producing [creating] too much of something. If there's too much it cannot be sold or processed further, resulting in wasted time and money.

Over-processing - performing extra operations that are not required by the customer. Such as painting a product red that doesn't need to be painted!

Defects - any mistakes that require either extra work to fix [to sort out / resolve] *or* result in scrapping [discarding] a product or item (throwing it away). Another word for defects could be errors. I think defects are what people most often think of when they think about waste in businesses.

When we talk about waste, we are often speaking of *ideal* world scenarios. In the *real* world it's almost impossible to achieve *zero waste* and *perfection*. One good example of removing waste was at a company where every product was thoroughly polished by hand before delivery to the customer.

The customers didn't need this because as soon as the product was run after delivery the polishing was gone! Removing this process saved millions of pounds (£m's) each year! This is a great example of over-processing.

A type of waste that is very difficult to avoid is called necessary waste. The main form of this is inspection or quality control. It's *necessary* because we need to ensure products are ok when they are delivered to the customer. Some companies may need to check one product in every million, whereas others need to check every individual part (the level of inspection required is often linked to the Six Sigma level of a process – the more scrutiny is required the more product quality is required too). Inspection is more important in industries such as aviation and medicine – where defective products can cause serious problems.

The Gemba

Now that we understand what waste is (and isn't), we can introduce the concept of the Gemba! Of course, as with a lot of improvement terminology, *Gemba* is another Japanese term which has no direct English equivalent. The Gemba can be defined as the specific process flow that delivers value to the customer. At each stage of a process you can ask "does this deliver value to the customer, or is it waste?" – or perhaps more precisely you can now say: "is this part of the Gemba or not?".

Remember that just because something isn't part of the Gemba doesn't mean it isn't necessary – it may fit into our earlier category of necessary waste. In a company that makes shoes, here's what might be considered part of the Gemba, and what might not:

The Gemba Summary Table

The Gemba	Not the Gemba
Shoe design and development	Purchasing department
Shoelace fitting to the shoe	Human Resources
Shoe packing	Factory Maintenance

Relatively few people are working in the Gemba but it is arguably the most important part of any business. Focusing on the Gemba as a first step in understanding the business is strongly recommended.

Go-Look-See

Our first step might be to go look at the process – by undertaking a go-look-see. The best place to do this (if unsure) will of course be at the Gemba (this is a specific type of go-look-see activity, sometimes called a "Gemba walk"!).

In a Go-Look-See you'll walk the process, typically from start to end. For a manufacturing business that could be starting at where raw materials enter and are stored in a factory, following their entry into the process and then after products are completed, viewing them shipped out at the end. During this process, you'll want to identify which areas are most important for business improvement focus – to do this the best thing to do is to look for waste. Here are my recommended steps for a Go-Look-See activity:

1. Walk the process from start to end
2. Highlight key waste areas against TIMWOOD
3. Draw and annotate a rough process map (covered further in the next section)
4. Walk the process again
5. Ask operators questions
6. Consider the key takeaways and areas for improvement

For each of the TIMWOOD waste areas, think about what you can see in the factory process. Additionally think about which processes are taking the longest. Ask yourself, which processes require the most labour? Which processes are creating the most waste? How clean and tidy is the factory?

Taiichi Ohno (yes, the same person who identified those wastes!) created a novel method of Go-Look-See where you draw a chalk circle and remain within it for many hours, simply "learning to observe" the process and spot waste. Time-wise, however, it's usually best to be able to walk through the process step by step in your Go-Look-See.

One final point about Go-Look-See which cannot be overstated is that however many hours you're spending observing a process, it's unlikely to be as much time as the people operating that process observe it for. So my advice here is simple; speak to them! Ask as many questions as you can and get as much information to understand the situation as possible.

I've created a rough template which can be used as a guide for a Go-Look-See which you can find in the appendices. See page 152.

Process Mapping

Process maps can take many formats and offer different levels of information. You should always complete a process map to the level appropriate – never more and never less. There are five key types of process map for us to discuss:

1. Basic Flow Chart (page 48)
2. Swim Lane Diagram (page 49)
3. SIPOC Diagram (page 54)
4. Value Stream Map (page 53)
5. Spaghetti Diagram (page 56)

Roughly, the first four in this list are given by order of complexity – spaghetti diagrams have a slightly different purpose to the others, as you will see shortly. If you're unsure of which type of process map to create, a good idea would be to start with a basic flow chart and carry on. In my experience, very few improvement initiatives require the completion of a full Value Stream Map.

The Basic Flow Chart

The basic flow chart is best for a very simple, quick overview of a process. You can use it to check understanding of a simple process between different teams and/or individuals.

For this example, I'm going to imagine a cake company and the process of producing cakes. Here's a rough idea of what a basic flow chart might look like for the Gemba of this organisation:

Basic Flow Chart Example 1

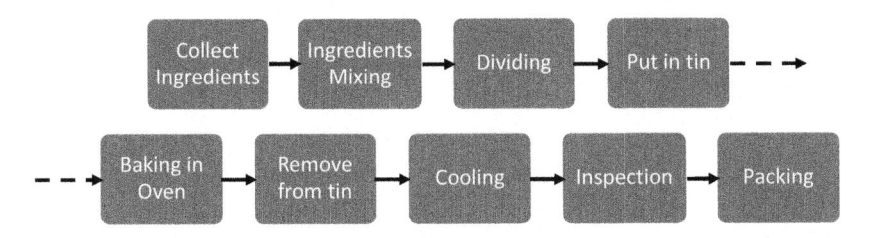

As mentioned above, you can make this process map as complicated as it needs to be. For example, perhaps you want to record the amount of people involved at each stage of the process, or how long it takes to complete it. Here's an example of how you might annotate it:

Basic Flow Chart Example 2

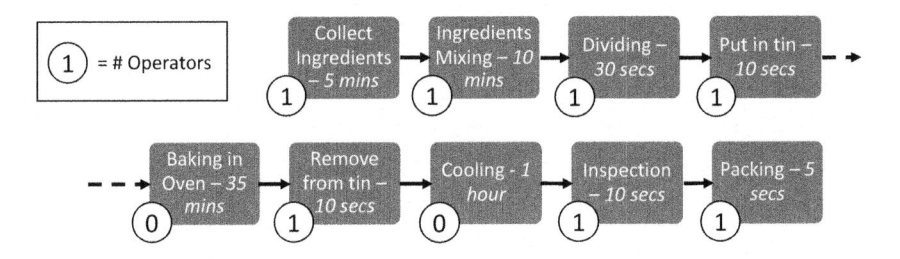

Swim Lane Diagram

It's often good to start with basic mapping to get a rough idea for the process. You can then, if required, move onto producing a swim lane diagram. A swim lane provides an appropriate amount of detail for around 80% of business situations. The "swim lane" is so-called because with this diagram you separate out the process steps into lanes, depending on which team or individual does a particular process step (see the example below after the instructions).

Here's the process for creating a swim lane process map:

1. Build your team

It doesn't need to be a big team – just make sure you have everyone you need that understands the different parts of the process.

2. Walk (or "talk") the process

Remember though – we're not just taking people's word for what the process is – we want to know the reality. Visibly seeing it in action – walking the process – is the best way to do that. Ask "what happens next?" as you move from one step to the next. It's often useful to think of all the question words and how they might provide further context: "Who?", "What?", "When?", "Why?", "How?". You can even bring a stopwatch and time how long certain process steps take.

3. Decide on your swim lanes

The answers to "who" is doing particular process steps form your swim lanes. The trick is to not be too vague but not be too specific either. Functions (such as "purchasing" or "finance") are often the right level for most swim lanes.

4. Build the flow chart

Use post it notes, whiteboards or flipcharts. Be creative! Bring everyone back together and put a draft of your process map together. When everyone agrees it looks right it's time to double check it. Remember you can use colour coding and add any additional information you might need.

Colour coding can be used to show whether processes are done in-house or external, or within different functions (if your swim lanes are more specific).

5. Validate the flow chart

Take a picture or print out of your new swim lane chart and walk the process again with that in hand – so that you can take notes on your map. You can now time the process steps (using a stopwatch) and ensure your work accurately reflects the current situation.

See the following page for an example swim lane diagram.

Swim Lane Diagram Example

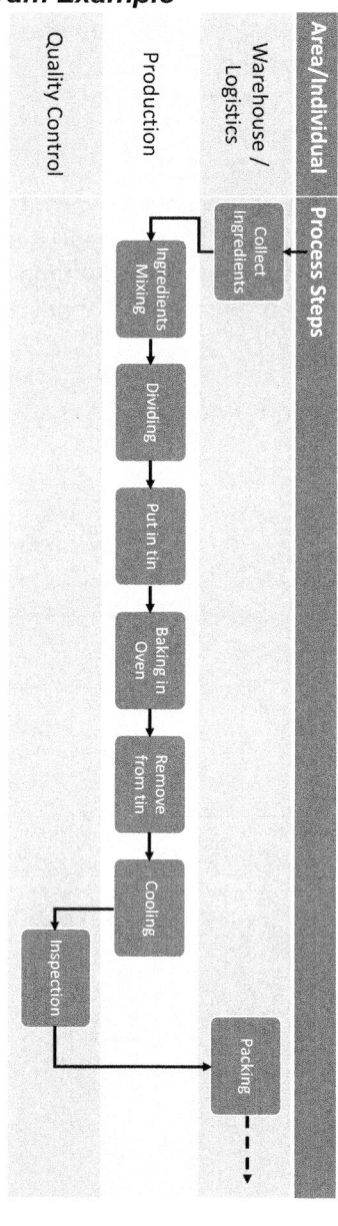

A key thing to look for with swim lane process maps is what happens at the transfer points from one team to another – where a product crosses a lane there are very often areas for improvement. For example, looking at the diagram above, I might investigate the handover from the warehouse/logistics team to the production team, after they have collected the ingredients (and before the ingredients are mixed). Likewise, it's worth looking at how the production team hands over the product to the quality control team for inspection after cooling.

Remember that whatever type of map you create, you can add any additional information that you might need to your map. Is it useful to know process times or batch sizes? Add them in! How about the number of operators working on a particular process? They can be added too! Don't be afraid to annotate the map as you see fit and through discussions with the wider team.

Value Stream Mapping

It is possible to take your process map to the next level of complexity (and therefore potential usefulness) by creating a full Value Stream Map (VSM). This looks at the whole business value stream from the supply chain through to delivery to the customer.

A key difference with Value Stream Mapping is that, after creating the current state map, part of the process is to create a future state map with what the process could look like – this allows you to create a list of potential improvements and draw up a plan of action from within your process mapping activities. It also means it's even more crucial that all your key stakeholders are involved from the get go. I recommend doing a more basic process map, like those above, or a SIPOC (below) first. If you can understand where you can improve through a gap analysis instead (see page 74), this is usually a more efficient process than putting too much time into a VSM at the outset.

SIPOC

A SIPOC is a different, tabular way of collecting key information for a given process. SIPOC is an acronym standing for the following:

- Supplier(s)
- Inputs
- Process
- Outputs
- Customer(s)

The key elements of the above are the Inputs and Outputs, allowing careful considerations of what the requirements are for each process step. Also the suppliers and customers allow for a clearer idea of what the boundaries or scope might need to be for a potential project looking into this process (for project scoping, see page 133).

A SIPOC starts having already created a basic process map, which is rotated and placed vertically in the centre of a SIPOC table. Ideally, alongside the wider stakeholders and team, you can brainstorm the key inputs/outputs and suppliers/customers for each of the process steps. See the example on the following page:

SIPOC Diagram Example Table

Suppliers	Inputs	Process	Outputs	Customers
Raw Material Supplier Companies	Eggs, Flour, Butter, Flavourings, Large box	Collect Ingredients	Large box containing all ingredients to correct quantities	Production Team
Warehouse / Logistics Team	Ingredients in correct quantities	Ingredients Mixing	Cake batter mix	Processing (Production Team)
Ingredients Mixing (Production Team)	Cake batter mix	Processing (Prep / Baking)	Individual, finished cakes	Quality Control Team
Production Team	Individual, finished cakes	Inspection	Individual, finished cakes	Warehouse / Logistics Team
Quality Control Team	Individual, finished cakes. Packaging.	Packing	Individual packaged cakes within larger boxes.	Distribution team (for delivery to end customers)

The process may need to be simplified (as it has been above) for a SIPOC. This helps to indicate the specific areas undertaken by different teams. It's intended as a high-level introduction to a process to understand scope, so it should be kept as such.

You'll also notice that a lot of the time, the inputs for one process match the outputs of the former. In fact, if they don't match exactly, this is another area that should be investigated further – perhaps one process is producing something that isn't adding value (and is therefore waste). In the above example, we can see that the output from Collect Ingredients includes a large box, not actually required for the Ingredients Mixing stage. This might lead to discussion around whether the box can be eliminated; is it possible to transport those ingredients another way or store those ingredients right next to the mixing step?

To take the SIPOC to the next level, you can identify what the key quality requirements are for each of the requirements. For example, perhaps each cake should weigh exactly 50g after "Processing" or maybe there should be 10kg of flour for each large box after "Collect Ingredients". These annotations should be added to the outputs.

Spaghetti Diagrams

Unlike the previous process mapping diagrams, depicting the process flow, spaghetti diagrams allow a different perspective, by focusing on the physical flow of material and products. Spaghetti tools can allow you to understand how the layout of a factory or office might be improved.

To create a spaghetti diagram, firstly draw out a diagram of the workspace you want to investigate. If it's a factory floor you may be able to print out plans detailing the locations of different machines and work cells etc. Take a physical copy of this diagram to the work environment and follow the product on its journey from start to finish. Don't just take someone's word for it – actually follow the product – this will ensure accuracy. You can repeat this step a few times to make sure that you capture the most likely or common route (ideally, if standardised, there should of course be just one!).

You should end up with something like the below:

Spaghetti Diagram Example – Current State

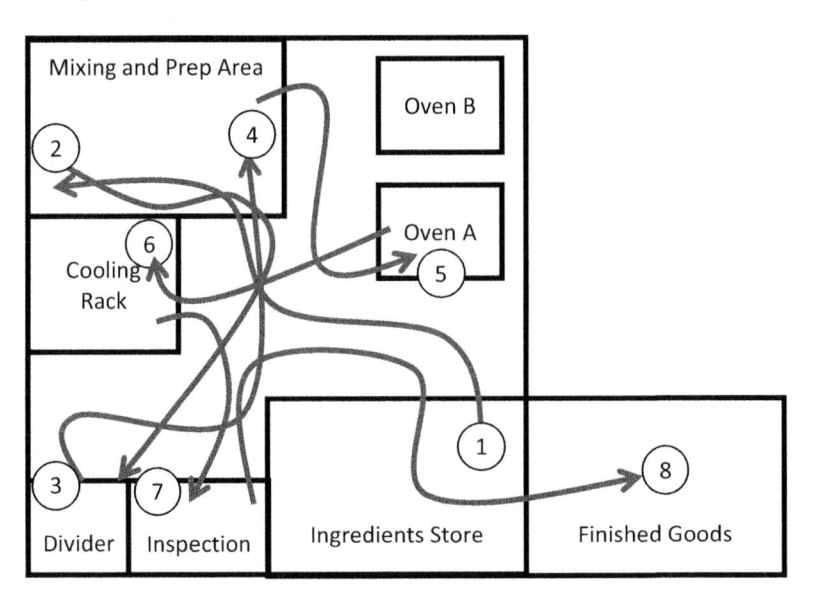

This diagram can then be discussed with the team, using brainstorming (page 93) and other problem solving techniques to think about how it might be improved. What we're looking for generally is lots of over-lapping lines, indicating that simplification might be possible. Of course, in an ideal world, all the processes in a factory can be in order, in a line. In reality, however that might not be possible.

After a successful project, you might end up with your diagram looking more like this:

Spaghetti Diagram Example – Future State

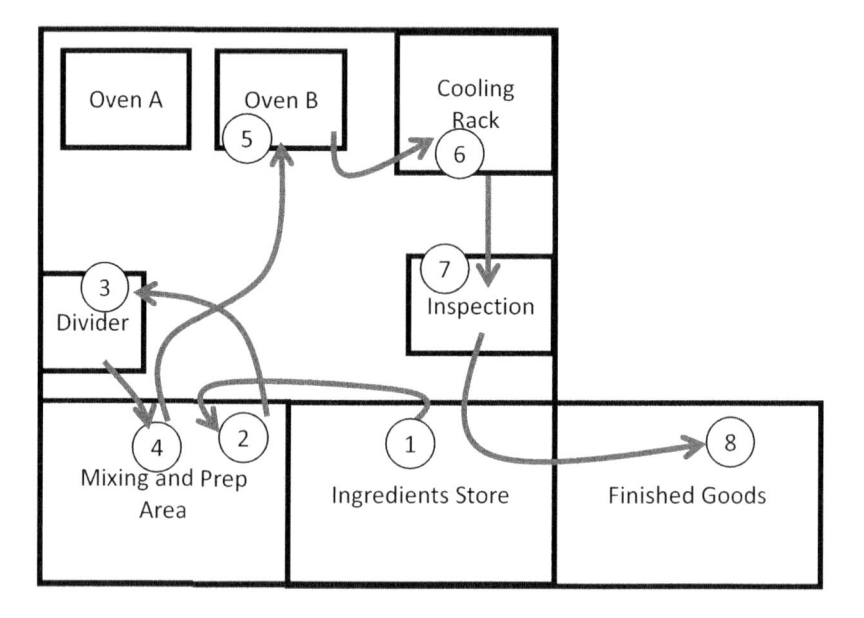

Voice of the Customer

As well as seeing and understand from an internal perspective, it's very important to get an external viewpoint – and none of those are more important than the customers' perspective. It is the Voice of the Customer (VOC) that is most important due to the Lean principle – the customer defines value.

There are two points at which gathering the customers perspective(s) is particularly important:

1. During the understand phase, to understand wider business issues and pain we are causing the customer
2. During individual problem solving projects, where we may mean customer in a more local sense (e.g. the next process step), to find out how this problem impacts its customer(s)

To gather customer opinion, you first need to understand what you require their opinion on. It's important to not limit any customer inputs to areas where you might expect more positive feedback (as happens all too often!). Some common ways to gather customer input include the following:

- Undertaking a survey (either an online one or via post)
- Formal conversations with a customer focus group or representatives (*structured* interviews)
- Informal conversations (in passing or in addition to already planned activities)
- Scope (for a project) or specification (for a product/service) checking with the customer – does your understanding of what's most important align with theirs

- Brainstorming (page 93) with the customer as to exactly what their requirements would be, if starting from scratch

Any of the above ideas could be used individually or combined with one another. Often from this, you're able to understand things from the customer point of view. If you are able to gain a list of key requirements (for a product line, project or for a business as a whole), I find it's useful to separate them into musts, shoulds and coulds.

- **Musts** – these absolutely *must* be delivered
- **Shoulds** – these *should* be delivered if there are the appropriate resources available
- **Coulds** – if everything else is delivered, and resources are still available, these *could* be added as well

Remember that you can't solve everything – sometimes the customer highlights issues that are too difficult (financially or otherwise) to resolve. Whilst looking at musts, shoulds and coulds works particularly well for customer requirements, it's also worth considering using an ease / effect matrix (see page 83).

Key Performance Indicators (KPIs)

How well a business is meeting the customer requirements is something of paramount importance to a business. This, and other important factors need to be tracked and understood day to day. To manage this, companies need Key Performance Indicators (KPIs), the *key* word here being *key*! You don't want to drown in data but instead to know when quick, decisive action is required – i.e. just to know the *key* information about performance.

Businesses select several key bits of data that help them make informed decisions and understand business or process performance at a glance. The best businesses have cascading KPIs; meaning that every level of an organisation has appropriate KPIs that feed into the level above. At the top of an organisation, for example, revenue (sales/income) might be tracked via the total number of products sold each day. To achieve this the purchasing department might be tracking the input materials, ensuring the required amount is delivered. Likewise, manufacturing will need to track the output products meets the expected demand. Specific teams should also have KPIs that help them meet the overall business targets. One further step that the best organisations take is to set individual employee objectives to be aligned with business KPIs – how can one person play their part in achieving business goals?

Going back to KPIs, there are five key elements that make a good KPI:

1. They are **based on valid data** – the source of the data is tested and proven to be accurate and reliable
2. They are **easy to understand** – the KPI has meaning to everyone who needs it

3. They are **actually used** (monitored and reviewed) – collected automatically or manually, it doesn't matter as long as it's regularly updated
4. They **measure something important** – going back to the *key* word we've already mentioned!
5. They use **SMART target(s)** (see page 91) – improvements are based around achieving certain levels against KPIs – it's no good showing it as green all the time when improvement could be happening!

Often, KPIs are standardised across a business, allowing quick comparison between different factories in a business. It's important that the way a given KPI is calculated is the same across all the different sites and is designed to derive the best possible value (as well as meeting the 5 points mentioned above). If you're not careful you can end up with a bad KPI:

Previously I remember a supplier reporting truck fill (a logistics KPI) by how many pallets were on each truck, out of a maximum of 26. Rather than fill each pallet as much as possible it became more important to simply put 26 half-full pallets on a truck! Other suppliers reporting only full pallets were penalised when actually they were being more efficient (as they reported a lower number of total pallets, yet carried a far higher volume of product!).

Other examples of bad KPIs include tracking the total hours a machine runs in a factory (rather than what it's outputting, based on what's needed). This meant that the factory had a preference for selecting products with a long lead time, over and above those that the customer actually wanted! In one final example, a popular UK supermarket set a strict KPI for its checkout staff of scanning speed, meaning staff threw items at the customer as fast as they possibly could; despite customers struggling with how quickly they were able to pack these items away. The result? The whole checkout and paying process took far longer than at other supermarkets not tracking checkout speed in the same way!

Additionally, KPIs can be leading or lagging indicators, meaning they either give information/clues as to what might happen (leading), or they tell us what has already happened (lagging). An easy example of this is in Health and Safety, where you may have come across the below pyramid previously:

Health and Safety Pyramid Example

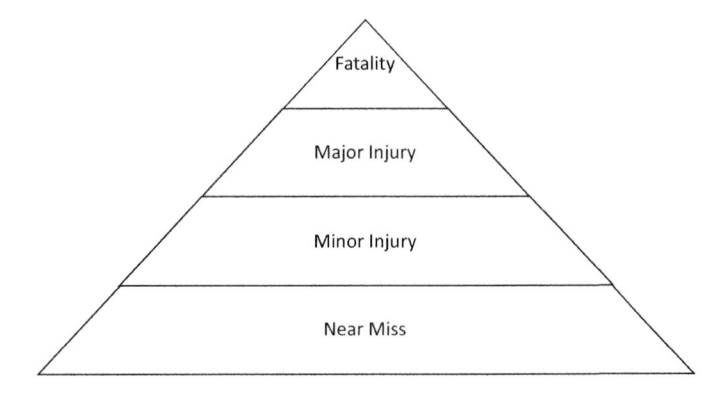

A KPI on near misses is a clear leading indicator to more serious injuries. If near misses are reported by all employees in a company, then action can be taken to understand and resolve these as issues. In companies not tracking this information, potentially the first they will hear about dangerous situations or practises is when a major injury occurs (a lagging indicator).

KPI's need to align with the requirements of a specific company – it's no good just copying what other companies do because it might not be relevant (and might not be the best way of tracking information anyway). Get KPI's right and you will have a powerful tool to reduce injuries and improve the efficiency of an organisation. Get them wrong and you might well cost the company more than if you'd done nothing. Use KPI's with care!

Quality Cost Delivery

Often, a way that company categorise the different KPI requirements, particularly in manufacturing (but just as much in a transactional environment) is to use QCD (Quality, Cost, Delivery). Some companies go two steps further and add S (Safety) and P (People). Within each of these areas, KPIs can be developed and seen at a glance. Ideally these will adhere to the points raised above – in particular needing to be visible and regularly (ideally automatically) updated.

So, for example, within a factory cell, a morning stand-up meeting might go through each of the SQCDP letters one by one, to provide crucial updates and understand what needs to be done going forward. Here are some ideas of what KPI's might be discussed:

Table of KPI Examples within SQCDP

Safety	Quality	Cost	Delivery	People
Number of near misses	Product recalls	Waste (% of total material cost)	On Time In Full (OTIF) %	Absence %
Number of accidents	Right First Time RFT (%)	Labour cost per unit	Number of orders overdue	Training courses completed
Safety concerns raised				

Of course, the above examples are just that – examples – every business and every area may need to develop their own KPIs to deliver on what they need to do, but the SQCDP framework provides a great basis to work from.

RAG (Red, Amber, Green)

"At a glance" understanding of KPI's is often driven by the use of simple RAG (Red, Amber, Green) colouring. The basis for what constitutes each of the colours needs to be agreed and understood in order to discourage what we might call *watermelons* (they're green on the outside but if you dig into the detail – they're red on the inside!). For the same reasoning, some companies don't allow an amber colour – stipulating that it has to be either red or green. As an example, a business might have averaged a Right First Time % of 90% over the previous year; meaning that the criteria might be set as follows; Green: >95% (e.g. 98%), Amber: ≥90% (e.g. 92%) and Red: <90% (e.g. 74%). As a company improves over time, these criteria should be regularly reviewed and, hopefully, track upwards to reflect this – setting new continuous improvement targets.

Run Charts

Run charts are a type of time series plot that show captured data in time order; i.e. the order in which they occurred. They are very useful to show how a process is changing over time, monitor the effect an attempted improvement (or other process change) is having, or to identify outliers – big, often temporary, changes that may indicate something is going wrong with the process.

We saw an example of a run chart earlier on in the introduction, here it is again:

Run Chart of Block Width Over Time

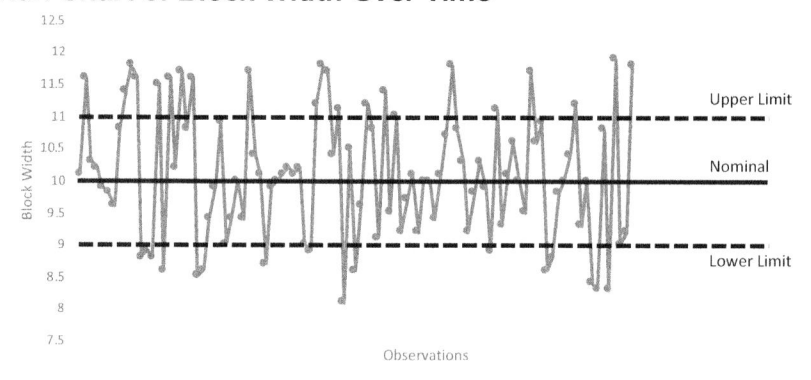

Adding tolerance bands (where appropriate) allows an additional level of information. This is useful for tracking how well a process is performing against its quality targets. The main thing we want to understand here is the level of variation (something we'll discuss further in the statistics section on page 119). Alongside a histogram (also in the statistics section), time series plots can tell us a lot about how a process is performing and also give us clues as to what might need improving.

Take a look at the below example. Do you notice anything you may want to look at in more detail?

Example Run Chart of Final Product Weight

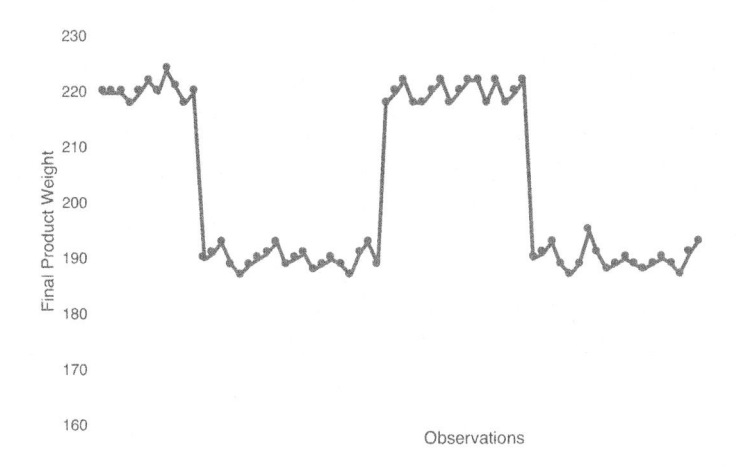

This is actually an adaptation of a real-world example. The final product (a food product) was found to weigh around 10% more when completed on a night shift to a day or afternoon shift. Completing a time series plot allowed the problem to be identified; operators on a particular shift were encouraged to fill the product more – perceived as being of benefit to the customer. In actual fact they were using more ingredients than had been planned for and costing the company money!

Production or Sales Constrained Environments

One of the key considerations when understanding the potential value of improvements is whether a particular business (or product) is production or sales constrained.

Sales constrained means there is limited demand for a particular product. This means that improving the company won't allow them to sell more products – only to make the ones they already do make better or quicker. Generally the goal here is to do more with fewer resources – typically by labour or time reduction.

Production constrained means that there is further demand for a product, but currently a company cannot produce enough. This is the ideal situation from an improvement perspective, because any recovered time can be used to make more products and therefore directly drive more revenue for the business.

As a rule of thumb, production constrained is worth around ten times as much as sales constrained (i.e. value of extra sales is worth ten times more than labour reduction).

Overall Equipment Effectiveness (OEE)

Overall Equipment Effectiveness (OEE) is a very common and useful type of KPI used in business improvement. It measures how well a manufacturing operation is doing when compared to its full potential – the percentage of manufacturing time that is actually productive. Therefore, 100% OEE can be said to mean perfect production.

OEE is a combination of three key factors; Availability, Performance and Quality. Each of these should be calculated separately and can then be multiplied together to give the overall OEE %.

$$OEE = Availability \times Performance \times Quality$$

The beauty of splitting it out like this is that we also get a good idea of where we might look first to improve our OEE (i.e. "which of the three contributing factors is performing the worst at the moment?"). First off, let's look at availability, this is the actual working time out of the total time scheduled:

$$Availability = \frac{Actual\ Working\ Time}{Planned\ Working\ Time}$$

So, for example, if our planned working time is 200 hours, but we had 52 hours of downtime, the actual working time is 148 hours. Therefore our availability is 74%.

Next, performance is calculated. This typically involves a bit more work as we need to understand how many products we could ideally produce – if we worked at the maximum speed for the entirety of our planned working time. Here's the equation for Performance:

$$Performance = \frac{Actual\ Products\ Made}{Maximum\ Potential\ Products}$$

Perhaps our maximum production speed is 10 units per hour. We can multiply that by the total planned working time (200 hours) to give us a maximum output of 2000 units. In this example we'll say we actually made 1200 units – so our performance is 60%. It's important to ignore whether these products are right first time (i.e. the 1200 units should *include* scrap and rework). We'll take account of the other products separately (scrap and rework) in the next calculation – for quality.

Quality is the last part of the OEE equation. This is calculated by dividing our actual products made *right first time* by those that were scrapped or required rework, added to the total actual products. As follows:

$$Quality = \frac{Right\ First\ Time\ Products}{Right\ First\ Time\ Products + Scrap + Rework}$$

Ok so we know our actual products made is 1200 units, let's say that 410 of those were either scrap or rework; giving us a right first time total of 790. Our quality is therefore 65.8%.

Now we have our availability (74%), performance (60%) and quality (65.8%) figures, we can combine them (by multiplying them all together) to get our total OEE figure. In our example our OEE figure is 29.2%. Actually, this is a particularly bad OEE figure!

Roughly, we can suggest a league table for OEE figures:

OEE Figures "League Table"

OEE	Comment
100%	Perfection
>80%	World Class
>60%	Standard
<60%	Poor

What the above examples don't give you is an idea of how difficult gathering all of this required data might be in the first instance. You'll need to ensure that all the planned hours are properly recorded and collated, whilst also relying on operators or production staff to properly record any non-productive hours, rework or the time taken to resolve issues on the shop floor.

OEE is worth doing though – once you understand all the constituent parts, you're a long way towards understanding where the business needs to improve. It can also give you a target OEE to aim for too, perhaps as a KPI (page 61).

Gap Analysis

Understanding the business as a whole is great, but at some point we need to think about narrowing it down – what should we actually focus on. For this we need to look at the data – starting at a company-wide view. We need to understand where the gaps are that we can hope to reduce. This activity is known as a gap analysis.

Do we have any data, perhaps from finance or another department, which can help us to uncover some key areas of waste? Typical areas we can look into include yield (i.e. material input vs. material output), spend of different teams or costs of certain processes. The key, as always, is to talk to people in the know and see what can be uncovered.

For a typical gap analysis, we can consider some key areas of typical business waste as discussed above in the OEE section. These are;

1. Availability – amount of downtime in a process
2. Performance – amount of output from a process (this is sometimes called speed loss)
3. Quality – rework or scrap products.

These three collectively capture everything for improvement in a manufacturing and equipment setting. Using the same data as we saw in the OEE section (page 71), let's put that onto a set of simple stacked bar charts (note the different y axis scales):

Gap Analysis Bar Charts – OEE Measures

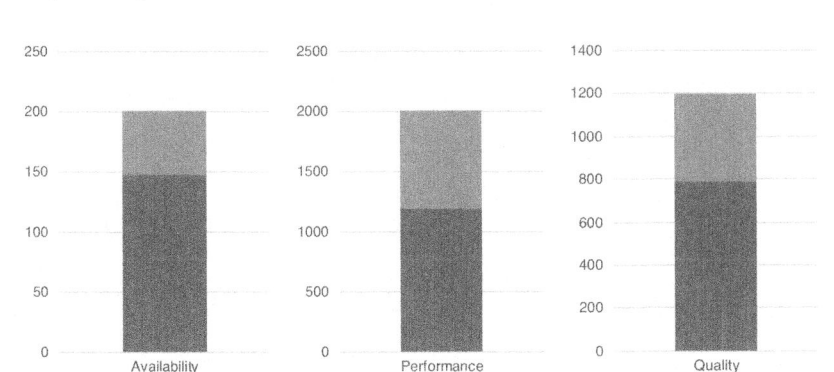

The top section of each of these stacked bars represents "the gap" available to us to improve. The difficulty comes in needing to be able to compare all of this using a common unit of measure. In almost all cases in business improvement – the best common measure is *cost*. Showing the values in pounds and pence (or dollars and cents) gives a common language that everyone in business can understand – it also allows for better decisions of which problems deserve the most attention (which is costing us the most?).

So, converting the above to cost will allow us to put these on the same graph (same y axis) and understand what our biggest area of opportunity is. As an example, when we convert for cost, this might be what our different areas now look like:

Gap Analysis Bar Charts – The Gaps in Cost (£) Terms

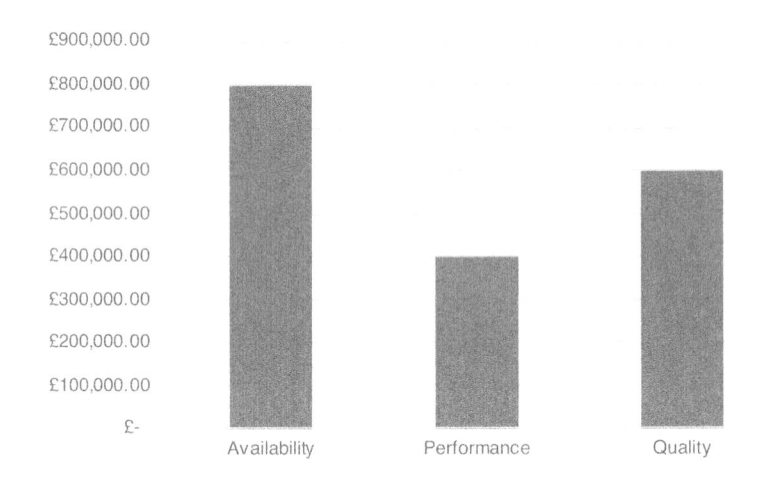

From the above, the first area we would look at would be availability. So we would want to know; what's driving our downtime? The next step for this is to break it down further and often, the best tool to do this is a Pareto chart.

Pareto

The Pareto chart derives its name from the Pareto Principle, based on Italian economist Vilfredo Pareto's 19th / early 20th century observations that 80% of the wealth of Italy belonged to 20% of the population. It's proven a remarkably versatile rule; with global wealth distribution thought to still follow a similar pattern today. Different studies in a variety of fields have also found this same trend. In mathematics, the Pareto Principle is known as the 80-20 rule.

In business improvement, we'll often find that 80% of our waste is driven by 20% of our problems (though, of course, this isn't *always* the case, it's just a rule of thumb). The Pareto chart can help us to visualise this, and is an excellent way to break down an area of losses.

In the previous example, using our OEE investigations and Gap Analysis, we found that Availability – the amount of downtime within a process – was our biggest gap. This had an impact of £800,000. Next, we can use a Pareto chart to break down this figure to see what makes it up. How does this figure break down into individual categories, elements or variables?

To create the Pareto chart, it's worth reiterating that we need to make sure, once again, that we're using the same unit of measure. As a first instance it might be worth just using a simple count of the number of errors recorded in the different categories. If we're unsure what categories to use then it's back to our process mapping (page 48) and consulting the wider team to understand where issues are coming from. It might involve timing, weighing or photographing parts of the process. We may even need to put new measures in place to understand things further before we can proceed.

Once we've gathered our data, it will look something like the below (ordered from largest to smallest):

Pareto Chart Data Table – Downtime Reasoning Counts

	Count	%	Cumulative %
Human Error	483	79.97%	79.97%
Software Failure	76	12.58%	92.55%
Unavailable Inventory	32	5.30%	97.85%
Hardware Failure	9	1.49%	99.34%
Cleaning	4	0.66%	100.00%

When we plot this data onto a Pareto chart, we have two y axes on the same diagram, one for the columns counting the data ("Count": displayed as a bar chart), and the other for the cumulative percentage ("Cumulative %": shown as a line graph):

Pareto Chart of Downtime Causes

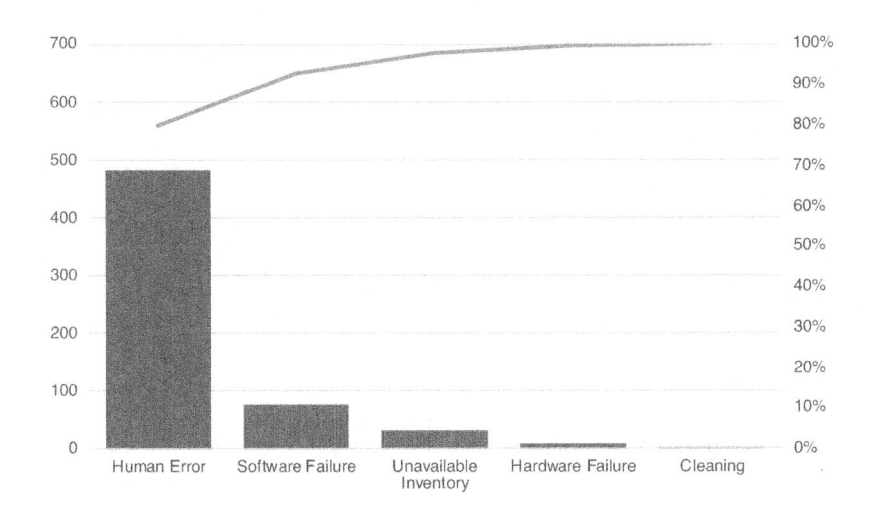

This shows that human error, in this instance is the single largest contributor to our issue with downtime (also, conveniently, this sits at almost exactly 80% - as the Pareto principle would suggest!). Now we can gather more data and break it down further, to get to the next level of information and find out what are the main causes of human error. The process is not dissimilar to the Five Whys (5Y) method (page 98) in that we are continually breaking it down to understand what the root cause is and how we might fix that – in order to have the biggest impact we can.

Pareto Chart of Downtime Human Error Causes

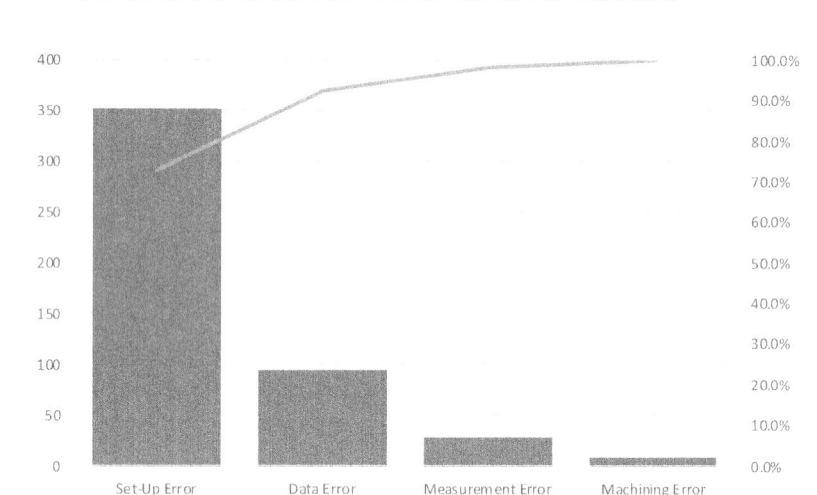

Now we've got to this stage, we'd probably say we need to look at an improvement project on operator set-up. A quick word on human error: it is not necessarily the "human" at fault! We should first look at the process that person is operating in and blame the process – not the person. In this example, I'd now want to look at the Standard Operating Procedure (SOP) (see page 113) being used and whether it's being followed appropriately or if it needs changing. Then I'd look at some other potential options within the hierarchy of control (page 110)– ideally error proofing (page 111) – to see if we can remove those set-up errors.

Remember that we are certainly not limited to using Pareto charts just for OEE style metrics. The Pareto chart is a very versatile tool. Take another example; in a food factory perhaps we have an idea of the overall kg of food waste produced on a weekly basis. We can Pareto this in order to see what might be the best area to focus on:

Pareto – Food Waste Example

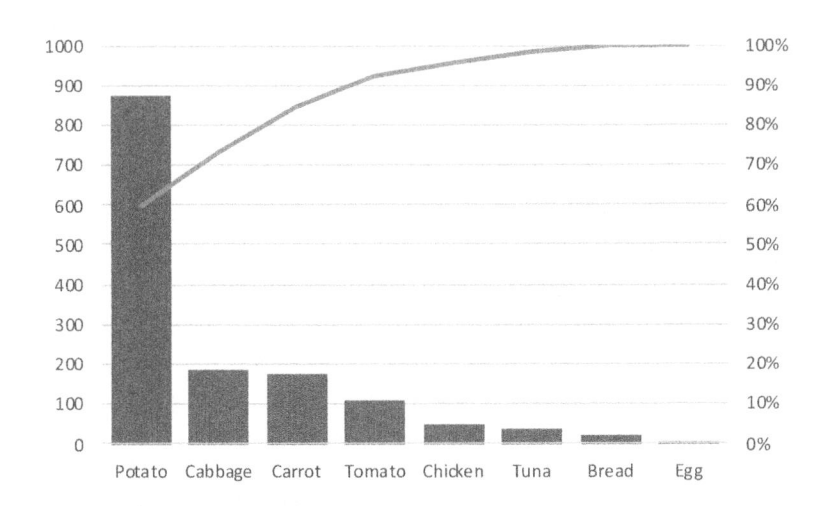

Following the above Pareto, as before, we can narrow this down further and look at the next level. What is the cause of our Potato waste?

Pareto – Potato Waste Example

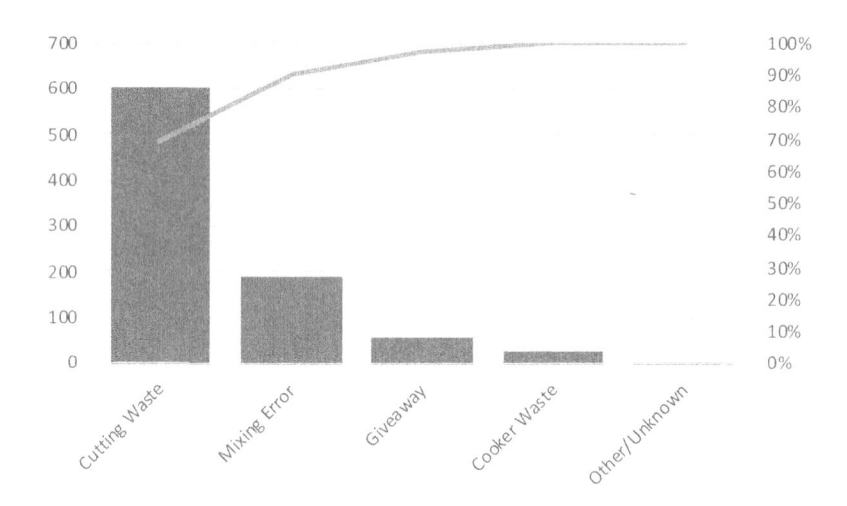

So then we might now reasonably decide to focus our attention on looking into the causes of Potato Cutting waste. In some instances a Pareto might be broken down to another level of detail before we get to a problem that needs solving. Using Pareto charts in this way helps to visualise a problem area, and works well alongside the five whys approach (page 98).

Ease / Effect Matrix

From completing process mapping, completing a gap analysis and Pareto charts, amongst other things, we would now have a large list of potential projects that we can focus on. A good way to decide where to look first is to complete an Ease / Effect Matrix.

A list of projects or initiatives can be scored (usually out of 10) against both ease (how easy it is to complete it) and effect (how effective the project would be – normally how much money it would save). This isn't an exact science and it's best to do this as part of a team to get a balanced view.

Once completed, the scores can be plotted onto a scatter plot, which can be roughly divided into four segments, as seen below:

Ease / Effect Chart Summary Example

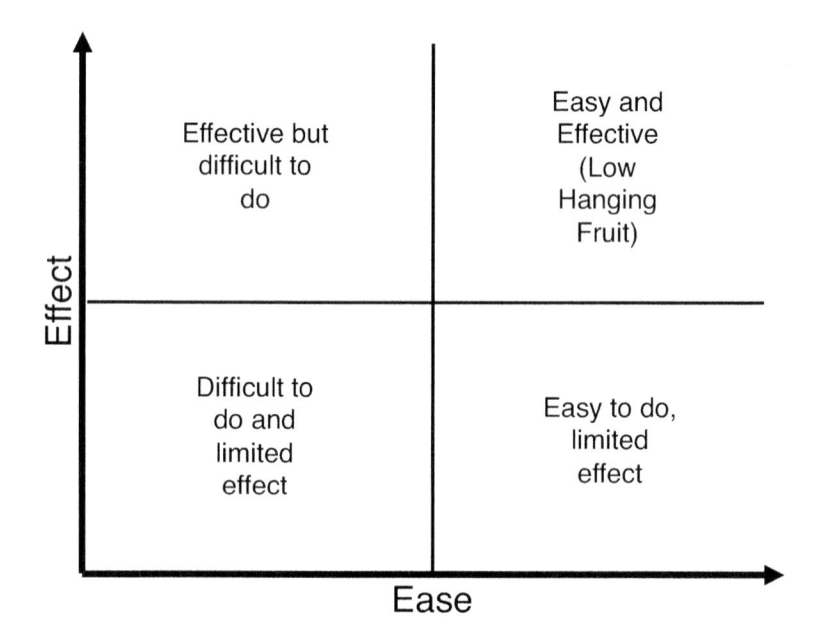

The top right are the projects we should focus on first – we can call these "low hanging fruit" (because they're the ones you pick first!). Typically there will be few projects in this area, and it'll be a choice between those that are easy but won't save much money, and those that will save money but are difficult to do. In my experience, it's best to have a mixture of the two – the easier projects can help to keep team motivation higher as they are completed, allowing the more difficult projects to be progressed over the longer term.

See below an example of how an ease / effect matrix might look in practise:

Ease / Effect Projects Matrix Example

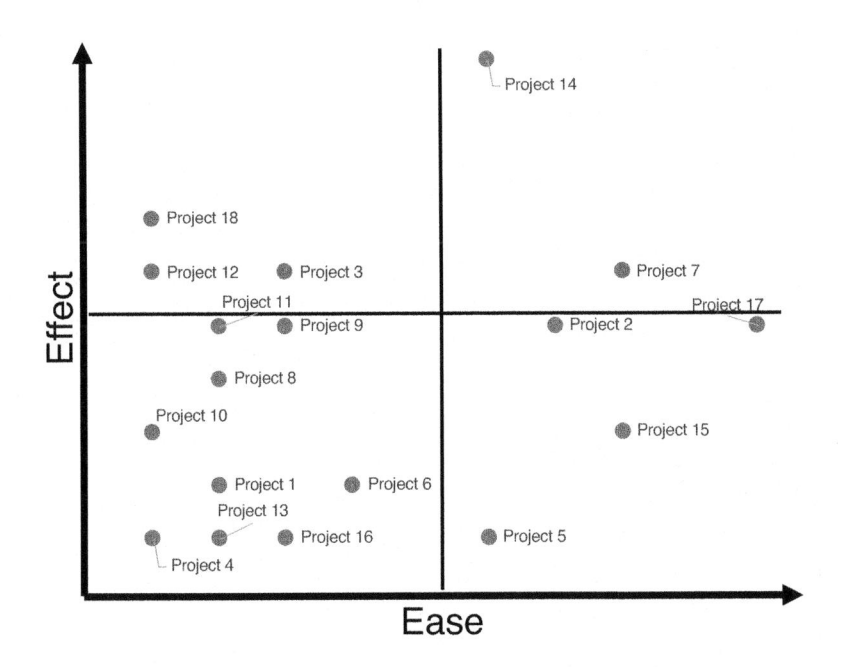

From this, we're lucky to have a few projects in and around that top right segment – we'll definitely prioritise Projects 14, 7, 17 and 2. Following this I'd look into Projects 3 and 15 next, before working our way down the remainder as time and team resource allows.

Failure Modes and Effects Analysis (FMEA)

FMEAs are a structured approach to identify where failures might occur and allow a targeted approach to preventing them. There are different types of FMEA, such as a Design FMEA (DFMEA), used during the design of a product, process or service in order to reduce failure risk. In business improvement, the most common and useful type of FMEA is used for already existing processes; the Process FMEA (PFMEA).

The PFMEA will, in addition to identifying potential failure modes, allow us to prioritise them by associated risk. A failure mode is the name given to any way in which the product or process will not be able to operate as it is supposed to do. The failure mode could cause later process steps to fail or be due to an earlier process.

1. Review the process on which we're undertaking the PFMEA. Consider creating a process map first (page 48) before proceeding.
2. Brainstorm (page 93) all the possible failure modes with the team.
3. List the effects of each failure mode – "what happens if…?"
4. List the monitoring and controls (page 110) in place for each failure mode
5. Add ratings for severity, likelihood and detectability (normally a score from 1-10 – note that detectability will be scored the opposite way around to what you might expect – the higher the score, the less likely it is to be detected)
6. Calculate the total risk score by multiplying the three ratings above

7. Order from highest risk score to smallest to show prioritised actions
8. Reduce or eliminate risk of highest priorities (via problem solving methods)
9. Re-score the PFMEA after changes to ensure the risk is now reduced

I've added an FMEA template to the appendices (see page 156). Below I've also added a quick example for the process of "making a cup of tea" on the following page. Note that as it's an example this is only partially complete to make it as quick and easy to understand as possible. Each process step would usually be looked at individually.

FMEA Table Example: Making a Cup of Tea

Process Step	Potential Failure Mode	Potential Failure Effect(s)	Current Monitoring / Controls	Severity	Likelihood	Detectability	Risk Score	Actions Required	Responsible (Name)	Date	Actions Taken	New Severity	New Likelihood	New Detectability	New Risk Score
Add hot water to mug	Water not warm enough	Tea is too cold	Visual inspection of kettle boiling	7	8	8	448	Retrain employees - pour water immediately after boiled	Person Name	04/11/22	Employees re-trained	7	3	8	168
Add hot water to mug	Water is too hot	Tea is too hot	Kettle automatic stop at boiling	8	1	1	80	N/A							
Add hot water to mug	Incorrect amount of water	Water spillage (overflow)	Visual Inspection	6	7	2	84								

The key take away is that FMEA's allow an appraisal of what *could* go wrong. It's very important that once this is identified, particularly for higher risk scores, appropriate action is decided upon and taken. These can be simple steps of monitoring and controls such as an update to training and/or an SOP (page 113) or it could be the start of a problem solving process or wider business improvement project.

The Problem and Goal Statements

Every business improvement project needs to be properly defined. If we don't know exactly what the problem is or what the goal is then we cannot proceed in the most efficient way.

With this in mind, there are two statements we need to create before going any further with an identified problem:

1. The Problem Statement
2. The Goal Statement

The Problem Statement

For the problem statement we want to identify exactly what the issue is. This should be quantified with measurements and data, be concise (not too wordy) and should not identify or suggest any causes within it. The problem statement needs to define what the "gap" is, using timeframe, location, any trends (if applicable) and clearly demonstrate the impact (cost).

Here are three example problem statements, which do you think is right?

1. For a year, 8% of one of our products failed inspection. Costing the business £240,000.
2. From June 2021 to June 2022, 8% of Product A failed at visual inspection after machining. This led to a rework process costing £200 per component (£240,000 in total)
3. From June 2021 to June 2022, 8% of Product A were deemed to fail at visual inspection after machining – most likely because of width machining failure. This led to an expensive rework process costing £200 per component (£240,000 in total).

The first example is clearly a little bit too short – we don't know what inspection has been failed or which product failed it! The third example also isn't viable because it's unnecessarily wordy and subjective (using words like "deemed to" and "expensive"). Furthermore this third example suggests a root cause before we've even started with the project – attributing it to width failure. Therefore the right option for a problem statement with this example is the second one – adhering to the rules laid out above.

<u>The Goal Statement</u>

The goal statement needs to be linked to the problem statement – this is, based on the problem we've now clearly identified, where we want to get to. Again, this shouldn't be too wordy and should not suggest any solutions. It's important to bear in mind the SMART acronym here too, meaning that the goal statement should be:

- Specific (one clear outcome)
- Measurable (we need to know when the goal is achieved)
- Achievable (not set up for failure – actually *doable*)
- Relevant (related to the problem identified)
- Time-Bound (clear time target for the goal)

I think of the above, the key one to bear in mind for a goal statement is *Specific*. If, for example, a problem is identified with the number of errors with a component, and those errors are split into different areas (also see the Pareto section on page 77) it would be prudent to focus on the area causing the most pain. Therefore the goal should reflect that.

Here's how the goal statement should look for the same example as we've looked at for the problem statement:

- Reduce the Product A visual inspection failure, after machining, from 8% to 4% by 31st January 2023.

This statement is short but effective. It specifies a clear goal (moving from 8% to 4%) and a timeframe that it should be completed in. It also mirrors (uses the same measures as) the problem statement above.

The problem and goal statements are key at the outset of any problem solving or improvement project – they're used as part of the project charter (page 131) as well as being used to define a problem in the 7-step process (page 102).

Brainstorming

An often-overlooked part of a business improvement toolkit, effective brainstorming is key to thinking of solutions to problems or even what might be a problem in the first place. This skill is also very useful outside of business improvement too!

Brainstorming is useful in solving problems but is better for free-flowing idea generation than it is at driving out a specific root cause. Brainstorming can be done individually or as a group, with the latter recommended, as always making use of the key stakeholders to help with a business improvement project.

Brainstorming can also be structured – perhaps using it alongside techniques such as the Five Whys (page 98) and SCAMPER (page 100) Often, good facilitation of a brainstorming session involves participants actively listening and the premise that "no idea is a bad idea". Quieter participants should be encouraged to participate where possible, while those who are a bit bolder or louder can be asked politely to allow others to share their thoughts too.

Some tips or options for a great brainstorming session:

- Go-Look-See
- Think outside the box – crazy can be ok and lead to further ideas
- Change the surroundings
- Break it down – one part at a time. As with problem solving, or any project, breaking it down into separate components can make the whole thing easier to handle.
- Use a tool – e.g. an Ishikawa or SCAMPER

- Quantity over quality
- Review and combine
- Listen to everyone, involve everyone

Sometimes participants might be asked to brainstorm individually in advance of a wider session. In this instance, for individual brainstorming, I recommend the spider diagram approach, as a way of simply and quickly organising thoughts, without being too rigid a structure.

Spider Diagram: Brainstorming Example

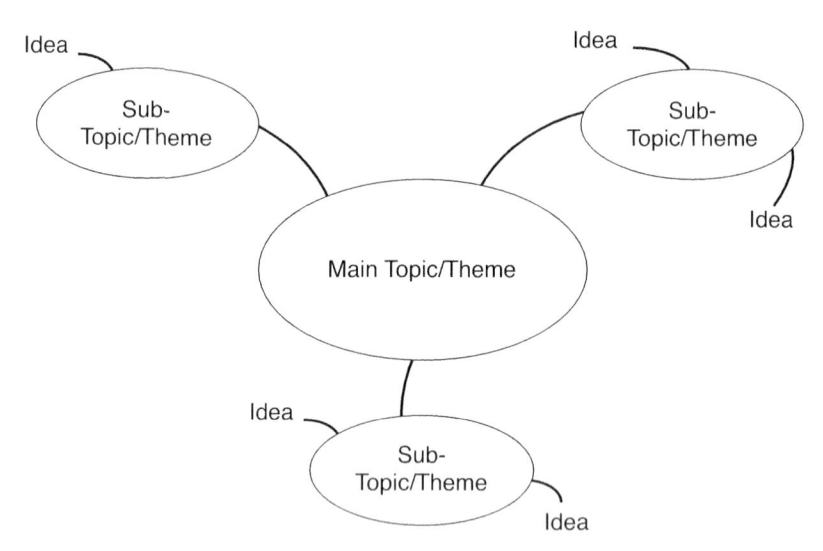

To create a spider diagram, simply select a topic and write it as a title in the middle of a blank page. I then draw a circle around it and think about what the next level(s) ought to be. Lines drawn outward to further circled titles can then be repeated to create the diagram and to catalogue all your ideas. Why not give it a go?

Ishikawa – Fishbone Diagram

The Ishikawa diagram (named for its inventor, Kaoru Ishikawa), sometimes known as a Fishbone or "Cause and Effect" Diagram, is an example of a brainstorming tool, used more specifically for identifying potential root causes. In my experience, the best option for completing an Ishikawa is as a group – using a whiteboard or large sheet of paper to capture the ideas.

The "head" of the diagram contains the name of the problem or issue on which we're brainstorming. The "bones" or branches of the diagram then form each area of investigation.

The six recommended categories for these branches are as follows:
1. People
2. Method
3. Machine
4. Environment
5. Material
6. Measurement

A useful way to remember these categories is to think of them as "6M" (with People being replaced with "Man" and Environment with "Mother Nature"). These six categories are only a recommendation – if you can think of other options more suitable to the particular problem you're working on – they can be changed. Below is the layout of a typical Ishikawa diagram:

Blank Ishikawa Diagram Example

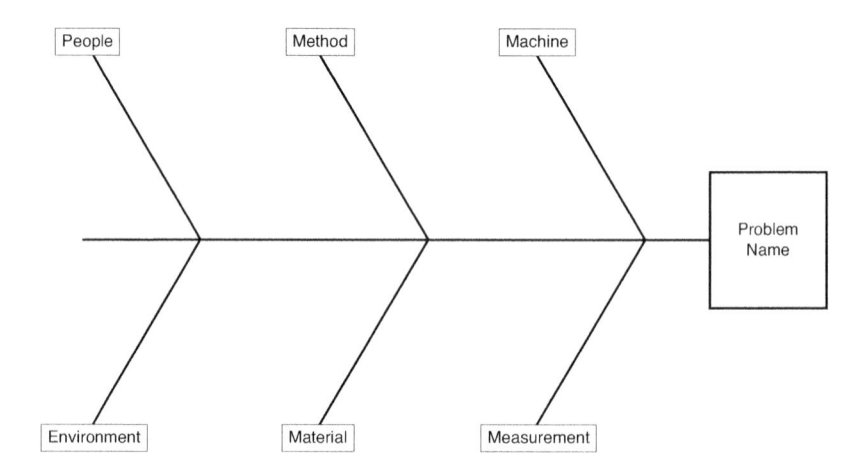

Each branch of the diagram can then be worked through and ideas given for what might be a potential cause of the problem. Here's what the diagram might look like after a brainstorming session for an example problem of some coffee being served too hot:

Ishikawa Diagram Example: Coffee Too Hot

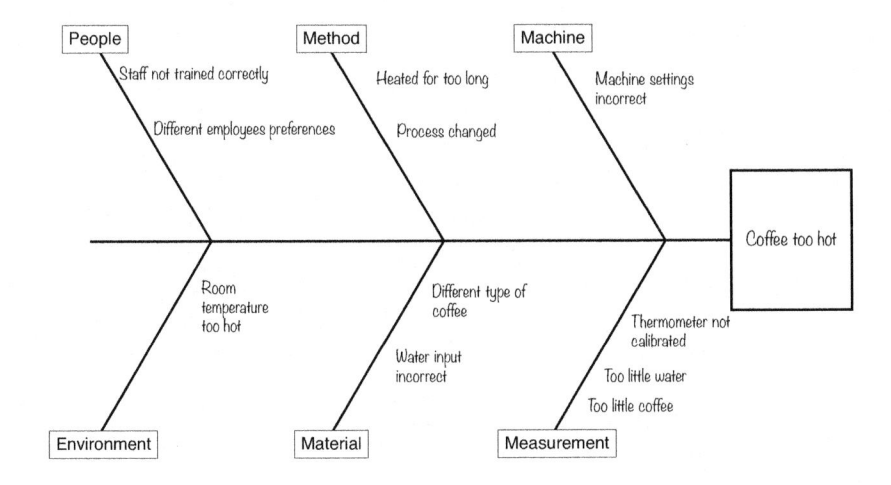

Five Whys (5Y)

The Five Whys (5Y) is another great tool to try and get to the root cause of a problem. It's another Toyota invention, by Sakichi Toyoda. The principle is that you cannot solve a problem with a sticking plaster, you must solve the true root cause to prevent it appearing again – this often means drilling into a relevant level of detail; often (though not always!) at or before the fifth level, the appropriate detail (and therefore root cause) has been found. The process of a five whys is fairly simple (assuming you have the right people around and have appropriately defined the problem beforehand):
1. Ask why
2. Ask why 4 more times

Ok, maybe the above is a bit too oversimplified, but hopefully the below example can bring this to life!

Imagine we're a sandwich manufacturer and we've had a complaint about "soggy sandwiches" from our customers. Firstly, we'll define the problem, and might come up with a problem statement like the below:

The moisture content of our sandwiches is too high resulting in customer complaints. This is affecting tuna mayonnaise sandwiches only.

1. Why (is the moisture content too high)?

There is too much mayonnaise in the sandwich

2. Why (is there too much mayonnaise)?

There is too much mayonnaise in the tuna mayo mixture.

3.   Why (is there too much in the mixture)?

The mayonnaise pouches are too heavy (overfilled).

4.   Why (are the pouches overfilled)?

The supplier isn't weighing each pouch before delivery (as they are supposed to as a critical to quality requirement).

5.   Why (aren't they weighing each pouch)?

The weighing scales are broken and there is a delay in a delivery of a new set.

At this point it could be taken further, but logically this seems like a relevant place to stop as it's clear that at this point, if we replace the weighing scales and ask the supplier to not deliver any overfilled bags, the problem should stop. We could ask why the weighing scales are broken or why there is a delay, but ultimately now it's apparent that there is a clear fix that can be applied here. Potentially we could also add a temporary weighing process prior to the tuna mayo mixing too.

It's worth noting that sometimes you might need to ask why one or two more times (or perhaps you don't need to ask why five times). The trick is to recognise when you are at the root of the problem; this something that will get easier with practise.

Sometimes, Five Whys is not able to get to the root of a complicated or difficult problem. In this case the method can still be employed and is likely to give useful insights – if not the actual root cause.

SCAMPER

SCAMPER is an idea generation technique – like a more targeted version of brainstorming specific to improving something (or solving a problem) once a root cause is known. For this reason, it typically fits within the "Improve" phase of a DMAIC project (page 33). The acronym for SCAMPER essentially provides a checklist for a team to develop new ideas and solutions. Here's what it stands for:

Substitute – can you substitute something from somewhere else? (Such as people, processes or materials)
An example of substituting might be to change the type of material you use to package a particular product – maybe swapping from plastic packaging to cardboard will save money.

Combine – can you combine certain features, processes or capabilities?
For example, mobile phones have combined with so many other bits of technology; becoming mp3 players, satnavs and digital cameras.

Adapt – can you adapt something from another process or product? Perhaps something from another type of industry?
A great example of this one is fast food restaurants taking Lean tools and manufacturing processes into a restaurant setting.

Modify – can you modify a function or product/process feature?
An example here would be in the fashion industry where certain features of clothing or accessories are exaggerated in order to help them to stand out and "be different".

Put to another use – can you use the same product/service in a different setting?
If parts for aerospace jet engines aren't up to specification, often they can be used instead in engines used in ground-based power generation.

Eliminate – can you remove something or a part of the process? Can this make things simpler or be worked round?
For example, some companies eliminate retailers by using the internet to sell their products direct to consumers.

Reverse – can you think about it the other way round? What might happen?
Often process steps don't have to be done in the order in which they always have been done, which in some circumstances means that you can free up both time and capacity.

7-Step Problem Solving

At this point in our run-through of the tools and techniques, we've learned enough to solve around 90% of all the problems we might encounter. Being more proficient at solving them will come with practise, but a handy way to put the problem solving tools together is via a 7-Step process. A quick search online gives many different options for 7-step or even 8-step processes (often, companies will adapt and create their own versions internally). The one I've written up here I believe gives a good balance and will allow us to draw on a few of the tools covered up to this point.

This process will show you how a lot of the tools and techniques we've looked at can be put into practice and be more powerful collectively than individually! Particularly for complex problems, the 7-step is best done as a team rather than as an individual. We'll build on this process further in the next section too by putting it into a one pager (page 106). But for now let's look at our seven steps.

See the following page for a flow chart of how to use the 7-step process:

Simple 7-Step Problem Solving Process

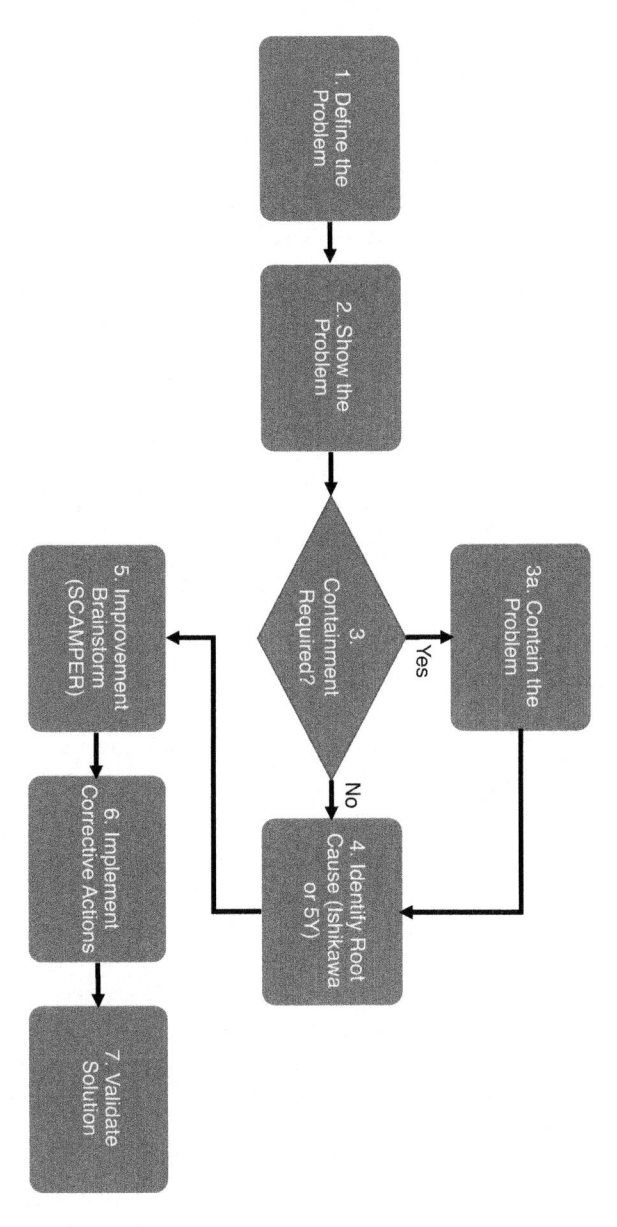

So, the first step is to define the problem. To do this we'll look at creating a problem and goal statement (page 90).

Once we've defined the problem, we want to *show* it. To do this, I like to ensure I understand the inputs and outputs surrounding the problem area (or process in question). A great way to do this is to create a process map – normally a simple flow chart will do (page 48).

Now that we understand exactly what the problem is, and the area around it, we need to think about whether a containment is required. Is the problem both causing immediate pain and forms part of a critical process? If so, it's likely we'll need to contain it before we continue. What we're trying to do here is prevent the problem escaping and causing more issues downstream (or even worse – being received by a customer!). Often, at this stage, an additional inspection will suffice (as the containment) to capture any issues. The problem is now contained. If it's not affecting delivery downstream or to the customer in an urgent way then containment can wait and we can move straight into finding the root cause.

To find the root cause, we can use the Ishikawa (page 95) and/or five whys (page 98) tools to identify them. If, at this stage, we're in need of a lot more data or information to be able to get to the root cause, it's likely that a simple 7-step process is not going to be able to resolve it. This doesn't mean our work to this point isn't useful though! If this were the case, we would take our understanding of the problem at this stage and use it to form a much wider improvement project, possibly in a DMAIC format and with a wider team to help in tackling the more complicated problem.

Hopefully though, we find that we are able to complete step 4 and know what the root cause is. Now I recommend using the SCAMPER technique (page 100) to brainstorm for a permanent solution to the problem.

Our solution(s) can then be implemented. A simple log of what the intended solution is, who should do it and by when should be created. The progress can then be tracked with a simple Red, Amber, Green (RAG) indicator (page 67). Something like the below works well:

Example Corrective Action Table

No.	Corrective Action	Resp.	When	RAG

Finally, when our corrective actions have been completed and the solution implemented, the final step is to validate that this has been successful. We'll come onto this again later, but it's particularly important to ensure that our solution is in place and permanent (see monitoring and controls on page 110), as well as ensuring our benefits are realised (see page 117). Of course if containment was required at step 3, validating a successful solution allows us to remove that containment at this stage.

That's it! All the key tools and techniques within one easy to follow process. The process is about to get even easier too, when we combine it with the one-pager approach next.

The One-Pager (A3)

Often a 7-step approach is combined with something called a "one-pager" (also called an A3 – for the paper size normally used!). The idea is that if you can't summarise it on one page then it's too complicated and is likely to be multiple problems (or a more difficult problem – as we've seen if you're struggling to find that root cause without needing a lot more data and insight).

A one-pager isn't just limited to the 7-step process; often businesses create a one-pager summary of particular projects that have taken place or other updates – especially for senior management visiting an unfamiliar area. The key idea is to be able to understand something "at a glance" – a concept not too dissimilar to KPI's (page 61).

To make problem solving even easier, I've created a 7-Step one pager, which you can find on page 160.

Single Minute Exchange of Die (SMED)

In manufacturing, often when an operation is performed, one product needs to be taken out and replaced with another, for the operation to be performed again. This process is known as a changeover. Changeover reduction can have a dramatic improvement on the time to produce products, especially at higher volumes. The process of reducing changeover times is known as a Single Minute Exchange of Die (SMED) exercise. This is because it was originally used (to great success) in changing the dies for automobile component manufacturing to be less than 10 minutes (so more "single digit" than single minute!). Here's the rough process for a SMED exercise:

1. Analyse and/or film the changeover
2. Break down into sub-processes
3. Categorise as internal or external (to the process)
4. Remove the externals, reduce the internals

The essence is to move as much as possible from the changeover to be an external process – what can be made ready prior to the need for a changeover, so it can be as quick as possible. The changeover should be analysed (ideally filmed and watched back) to break it down into its sub-processes. Always involve a group of key stakeholders. Each of the sub-processes can then be considered to see what might be done externally to the changeover – against each step, catalogue whether it's *internal* or *external*.

As an example, think of a Formula 1 (or motor racing) pit stop; more specifically the "changeover" of a car wheel / tyre. Firstly, we need to break down the process down – not just thinking of it as a single activity, but as a group of smaller ones. Gantt charts are a great way to show how the process breaks down. See example below:

SMED Gantt Chart Example: Wheel Changeover

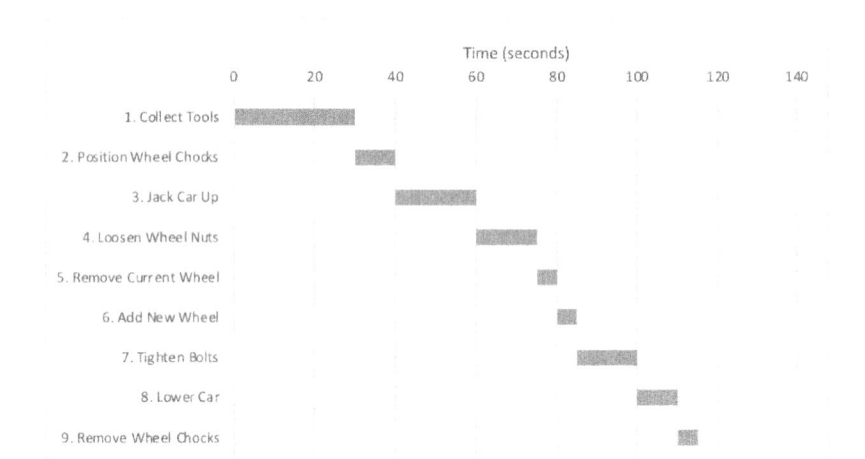

Now we understand each of these process steps and how long they take, we can think about how to reduce their timeframe. To do this we'll focus mostly on two areas:

1. The process steps that take the longest
2. Any steps that can be done externally to the changeover

At this stage, as with so many improvement tools and techniques, we would brainstorm with a team about how best to approach each of the above. As an example, we can see that the longest process steps are to jack the car up as well as to loosen or tighten the wheel nuts. Perhaps for these we can, instead of using a jack, use a device that simply pivots the car up to the ideal height. For loosening or tightening the wheel nuts – instead of manually turning with a wrench, we could invest in a pneumatic wrench instead, set to the exact torque required. At the start or end of the process, time might be saved by having all equipment and the spare wheels ready to go – collecting the tools being a perfect example of a process step that could be done externally to the actual changeover process. Furthermore, we could separate out particular parts of it by having different people doing different bits too. Perhaps one person places the wheel on while another is holding the pneumatic wrench ready to tighten the nuts.

The above example Gantt chart is roughly the timeframe motor racing operated within during the 1950s or earlier. Nowadays, thanks to SMED and changeover reduction, the whole process (for all four tyres – not just one) regularly takes less than 2 seconds! All of this is about making as much of the process external as possible – meaning preparation is done whilst time is less critical (i.e. outside of the critical path). Often in the manufacturing world this means whilst the previous part is still being worked on in a machine.

It's worth considering using this technique alongside SCAMPER (page 100) and Brainstorming (page 93).

Monitoring and Controlling

Any solutions implemented will likely need to be monitored or controlled in some way, at least in the short term, to ensure that problems don't reoccur and that any adopted solution is truly a permanent fix. To do this, we can use one or more measures from the so-called hierarchy of control.

The Hierarchy of Control

The hierarchy of control is something borrowed from an approach to health and safety – whereby something is altered to reduce injury risk in the workplace. In business improvement the hierarchy provides a list (in order) of which measures are best placed to control a root cause. Some of the measures are fairly obvious or self-explanatory (e.g. removing the need for something) while others need a bit more explanation (e.g. one-point lessons). Further explanations follow later in the section where required.

1. Remove the need for it
2. Error Proofing (Poka Yoke) (page 111)
3. Use of Colour Coding – for example, using the same colour for two parts that are joined together in an operation
4. Labelling and Signs – clear, effective visual management
5. Training – ensuring staff have practised and have the skills for a given operation (or change)
6. Inspection (checking that something is done or has been done correctly)
7. One-Point Lessons (page 112)
8. Standard Operating Procedures (page 113)

You will note that Standard Operating Procedures (SOPs) are at the very bottom of our list – they are actually considered to be the least effective control we can put in place. The reason is that simply changing the instructions or way a task is carried out is not enough to actually enact that change – i.e. instructions can always be ignored. Despite this, SOPs are often the one and only measure of control that a lot of businesses put in place (and then wonder why things go wrong!). SOPs should always be used alongside one or more other control measures. Always use as many control measures as possible.

Error Proofing (Poka Yoke)

Removing something (e.g. a process step) entirely isn't always an option. So the next best thing is to error proof (you may also have heard the Japanese term used; Poka Yoke). FMEA (page 86) should ideally have been conducted first to give a good idea of what exactly needs error proofing – it might be, however, that a root cause analysis has instead given us a very clear understanding of what needs to be error proofed.

Error proofing comes in many shapes and sizes and usually some level of innovation is required to find the appropriate solution. Whatever the solution, it boils down to three key steps:
1. Create an error proofing device – design and develop this new solution
2. Install the device – put the solution in place (in a controlled way)
3. Confirm that the device is working as expected – undertake trials as required

The best error proofing devices are often stolen (with pride!) from other industries or areas. For inspiration, here are some error proofing examples:

- Some types of fuel pumps are designed so as to prevent them fitting into the fuel tank for a car that does not use that type of fuel. I.e. the shape of a diesel pump nozzle will not fit into a petrol vehicle.
- Sink basins have overflow holes in them to prevent water leaking over the sides if a tap is left running.
- Dishwasher appliances stop operation if the door is opened – preventing spillages.
- Some online forms (for data entry) on websites will only permit certain types of characters or words (e.g. a field for an email will only allow a submission if it is structured like an email).

The best error proofing is often the simplest solution. If an oversize product or component was a problem, simply having a hole of some kind that it has to fit through can be enough to provide a solution (similar to a type of "go, no-go" gauge).

As a final point, it's important to note that, from an FMEA (page 86) perspective, whatever we put in place as the error proofing device becomes the new failure mode.

One-Point Lessons

A one-point lesson is a simple, visual description of a task or an *outcome* of a task. One-point lessons often (though not always) form part of a Standard Operating Procedure (SOP) – perhaps as an additional page of that document.

The most common use of one-point lessons is in showing what good and bad look like for a given product. For example if a process is toasting bread, a large red "X" can be shown above images of either burnt or under-toasted bread. Whilst a large green tick ("✓") can be shown above a picture of perfectly toasted bread. This makes it clear to everyone involved in that process what good looks like.

<u>Standard Operating Procedures (SOPs)</u>

A Standard Operating Procedure sets out the required steps to complete a particular process or task within an organisation. It sets a clear standard that should be adhered to, 100% of the time, to ensure standardised inputs and outputs for a given operation.

As discussed previously, an SOP is considered one of the least effective (though still important) measures within the hierarchy of control. This is due to the fact that although specific instructions are written down, human nature is always to find the most efficient way of completing a task. The trick here is to have engaged, improvement-aware operators, who recommend improvements to speed up a process rather than just doing them (and potentially causing variation and problems from doing so!). This means that regular go-look-see activities (page 46) are a requirement to ensure proper adherence to the process.

After an improvement project has been completed for a process, it's likely (if not almost guaranteed!) that the SOP will need to be updated. It isn't the most glamourous of tasks, but it is very important. The following are the approximate steps that will be required to update (or create) an SOP:

1. Stakeholders and Users
2. Template Check, Structure and Format
3. Collect All Information

4. Writing the SOP
5. Testing and Validating the SOP
6. Stakeholder Sign-Off
7. Implementation

Stakeholders and Users

Firstly, it's vital that the right people are involved in the updating of an SOP. For example, you may need to ensure representation of the quality control and operational functions as a minimum to ensure that both the users and the owners of the process are involved.

Template Check, Structure and Format

Next, check the template for the SOP – the first place to look will be (assuming there is one) the current SOP – is this in the best format to use going forwards? A good SOP should be clear and precise and not just show the step by step "how to" guide. It should also show a version number, an example of input(s) to the process, output(s) from the process, who does it and who validates it. When updating the SOP the whole document should be checked, even if only a small part of it needs updating. A new date will be added when the document is re-issued.

Collect All Information

Then, collect all the information required – if you've just done an improvement project on a given process, it's likely all of this is already to hand! Sometimes it's a good idea to take some pictures to help make the SOP as clear as possible – potentially creating and including a one-point lesson (page 112) which could show what good (and bad) look like.

Writing the SOP

Now it's time to write out the SOP – as mentioned above, check everything on the SOP is written properly based on your understanding, and add the updates required. If appropriate, involve the stakeholders and users at this stage too. The level of detail used here is key – ensure the SOP is both clear and concise.

Testing and Validating the SOP

Go to the process and run-through the draft SOP with an operator (somebody who will be *doing* the process in Business As Usual (BAU)). It's often good practise to run through the SOP draft yourself, perhaps whilst observing the process, before involving others. Once the initial test run-throughs you'll want to ask all appropriate stakeholders to validate that the SOP is accurate.

Stakeholder Sign-Off

Once stakeholders are happy, they can sign-off on (give their agreement to) the new SOP.

Implementation

To implement the SOP, you will need to check if any training is required – if so, that will need to be arranged (think about who needs to go to the training and who will conduct it). Perhaps there will also need to be a sign-off to show all operators are competent in following the process. As well as training, it's worth considering if any other measures from the hierarchy of control are appropriate to ensure process compliance.

Here's a rough idea of the format that can be used for an SOP (note that, normally, the top section is repeated on each page, whilst individual steps might take up a page each).

Example SOP Format

Process Title:		Version Number:	
		Updated (date):	
		Updated (name):	
Process Inputs:		Process Outputs:	
Step 1			
Step 2			
Step 3			
Step 4			

Benefit Realisation

Often when a root cause has been identified, and particularly when controls have been put in place, management are keen to get the resource back and focused on something else. However, we need to be sure that the benefits we set out to achieve, have actually *been* achieved. This is something very often overlooked when a difficult problem now disappears from everyday view, but it's something that's integral to ensuring value for money within business improvement.

To ensure benefits are realised, we need to go back to what we understood back at the beginning of our journey. A good place to start with this is to look back at our goal statement (page 91) again. This clear statement says what we should have solved and what we should have saved. The example goal statement used earlier was:

- Reduce the Product A visual inspection failure, after machining, from 8% to 4% by 31st January 2023.

So, at this point we'll now measure again over a time period, to ensure that the failure is at or below 4%. If it's not, we need to do more on this project. If it is though, we're ready to close out our project (and hopefully to celebrate and reward the team!).

An example of benefits realisation not being done properly is where an improvement project has reduced the amount of labour required in a process. We would need to go look again at that process and ensure that the labour has been removed. But crucially, is that labour no longer being paid for? If the individual is sat idle, not participating in the process then the benefits have clearly not yet been realised – the business (labour) cost for this process remains exactly the same. In this example, part of the benefits realisation in this instance may be to find another, value-add role for this individual.

Basic Statistical Analysis

As has been alluded to throughout the book, data is often fundamental to successful problem solving. It's about making decisions based on fact rather than opinion. Of course, the intention here is just to discuss at a high level some key statistical analysis and data points so that you can understand the basics.

Note that some of the key areas of statistical analysis have already been discussed, such as run charts (page 68) and Pareto charts (page 77). We've also looked at understanding some core terminology during the introduction chapter (page 35). If you're unfamiliar with statistics or data, I recommend reading these sections first before you continue here.

Variation

Often something that we want to identify is variation. Variation is simply the difference in whatever our process or business is outputting. There are two types of variation:

- Common cause
- Special cause

If a process only has common cause variation it is said to be "statistically in control". Every process has common cause variation. Though outputs from a process might be random, the variation is stable and predictable within a range – it always falls within certain boundaries (even though these boundaries might be above or below tolerance bands). To reduce common cause variation, new methods or procedures need developing – the same task may need to be done in a different way.

Conversely, special cause variation goes above and beyond common cause; driven by factors that are not always present in the process. It is said to be "statistically *out* of control". Variation might not be random, but it's difficult to predict when it will happen or how big an effect it will have.

The trick to reducing or removing special cause variation is to track down and eliminate the root causes for when the special cause variation appears. Run charts are often the best way to see variation in a process.

Data

Data collection and analysis is what statistics is all about. How to cut, slice and consider this data is a key skill for business improvement.

First off, there are two types of data;
- Continuous
- Discrete

Continuous data is generally the preferred option for analysis, this is data that can be infinitely divided – numerical data such as the lead time, width or length (anything really!).
Continuous data might look like this:

- 18.73
- 19.63
- 20.12
- 20.22
- 18.76
- Etc…

The other type of data is called discrete data. This is effectively anything else. It could be a basic count of

observations (e.g. 10, 2, 5), binary (yes / no) or using names of something.
Discrete data might look like this:

- Area A
- Area A
- Area C
- Area A
- Area B
- Area C
- Etc…

Whatever data we collect, it can be input or output. Ideally, we'll want the *input* factors that lead to a given *output* (to help us understand the root cause of a problem). Inputs could be the width measurement going into a process, followed by the width measurements coming out (the outputs). SIPOC diagrams (page 54) can be very useful for understanding what data can be collected.

This brings us onto correlation – understanding how closely related two sets of data are. For example, you would expect that the input width would correlate with the output width. Often, a quick way to test out correlation is to use a scatter plot – these can clearly show patterns in data. Often, if there's correlation you can see this through how the data is represented. If the data is closely packed together in a linear pattern (see example on the left, below), that indicates a stronger relationship than a more random appearance (see example on the right, below).

Scatter Plot Correlation Examples

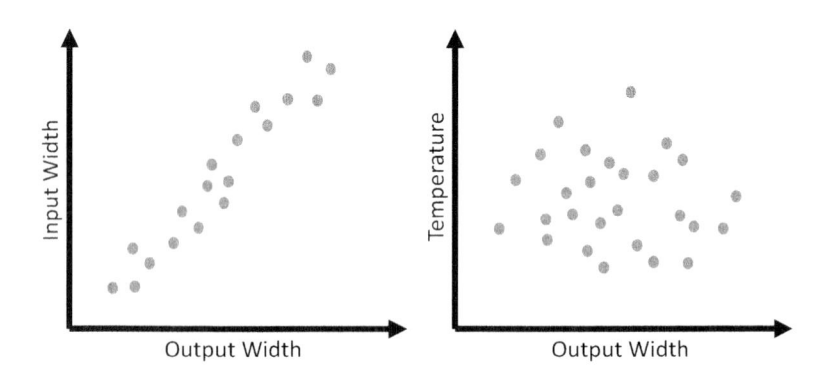

In order to create a scatter plot, it's important to note that data will need to be *paired* – i.e. an input is paired with its matching output. To state the obvious – if the data used to create the plots isn't paired (i.e. directly related), you cannot draw any conclusions from it.

Careful thought will need to be given to the best data for a given purpose. It might be that some required data isn't currently measured, so we'll need to arrange for that to be collected – either on a temporary or permanent basis. It's also worth noting that we need to be confident in the accuracy of any measurement system too – i.e. if we're measuring with a ruler, how accurate and reliable is that? Is it better to create a simple "go, no-go" gauge (a measurement tool at an upper or lower tolerance limit that a tool should pass – go – or not pass through – no-go) and collect binary, discrete data? These kinds of questions will often lead to a Measurement System Analysis to ensure it is accurate and reliable.

Data Distribution and Understanding

Once we've got a set of data, there are some key areas we want to be clear on as a starting point. To do this it's a good idea to use a histogram. We'll come on to histogram charts in a moment but initially let's just look at some key values that we'll want to calculate.

Understanding the *average* data point is very useful. There are four key measures for the average of data (sometimes referred to as the central data point):

- Mean – arithmetic average of a data set
- Median – midpoint of a data set
- Mode – most frequently observed result in a data set
- Range – the difference between the largest and smallest values in a data set (if I'm honest this is more of a measure of data *spread* than an average but it fits nicely with the others!)

There are some more advanced statistical measures for our data but we'll leave those for now and move on to look at some of this in action, specifically by looking at histograms. Histograms give a quick look at the spread and layout of the data – they're useful whenever we have continuous data to look at and can bring some of the measures we've discussed to life. Look at the example histogram below:

Histogram of Output Width

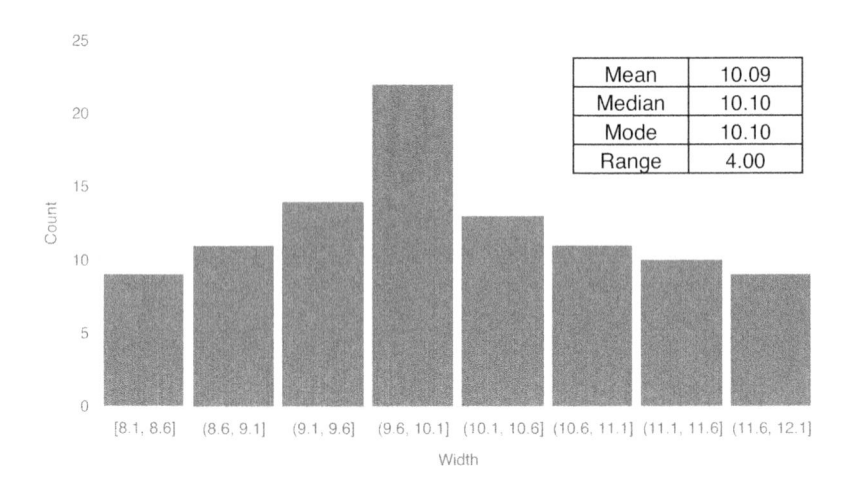

Mean	10.09
Median	10.10
Mode	10.10
Range	4.00

Rather than the y axis showing a recorded value, it instead shows a count of the total number of observations seen within a given category. The hardest thing with creating a histogram is to choose the size of the (non-overlapping) categories given on the x axis. Modern spreadsheet software can do the hard work for you these days saving a lot of time and effort.

In the above example the size of each segment is 0.5mm, so each observation within that range is given as one observation in the histogram bar. Looking at the measures of average and data spread (in the table, inset), you can see how they align to the histogram – the mean, median and mode all focus on the centre of the histogram, whilst the range clearly shows the difference between the upper and lower limits.

Not all data sets will have this nice (roughly) bell-shaped curve – indicating what is known in statistics as a "normal distribution". There are a few common histogram shapes to look out for, which indicate different types of data distribution;

and whether statisticians would say the data is normal or non-normal.

Histogram: Normal Distribution

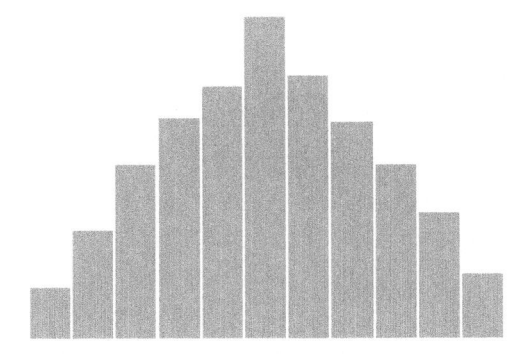

Firstly, this pattern (similar to the earlier histogram example) shows a normal distribution of data, with the data more or less mirrored either side of a central, mean column.

Histogram: Random Distribution

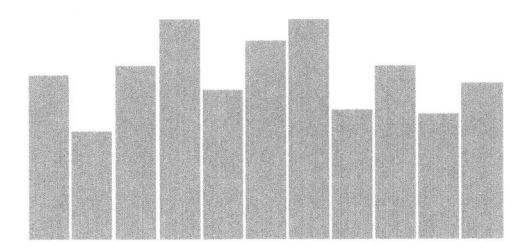

Sometimes, data can be very random (and definitely what we could call non-normal). It can be very difficult to perform appropriate statistical tests on this distribution of data.

Histogram: Bimodal Distribution

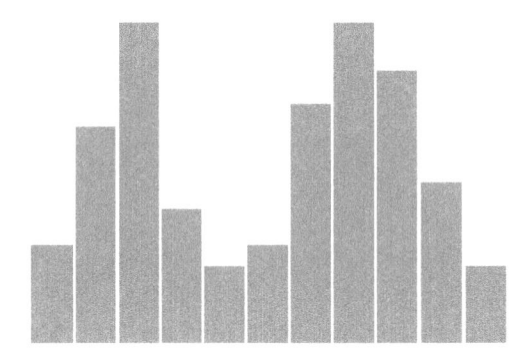

This example would be termed bimodal – also non-normal. This is an indication that there are two clear pathways through a process (see page 69 for an example of what this might look like on a run chart).

Histogram: Skewed Distribution

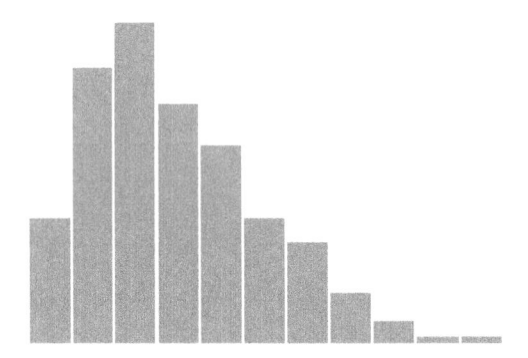

The last example would be called skewed data, where it is pushed towards one side of the histogram.

Statistically Verifying Causes

Normally distributed data is particularly useful for statistical tests to prove correlation between two samples of data (i.e. often, to prove that an input is statistically likely to have caused a given output). This is often needed to prove (beyond doubt) a particular root cause of a problem.

To prove that you've found the absolute root cause of a problem, especially if you're using continuous data, you will need to statistically prove (or disprove) one or more *hypotheses*. A hypothesis is a statement that can be proven to be either true or false (e.g. "the input width affects the output width of the block"). If, in this instance, we have normal data for both input and output width, we can perform a statistical test to prove or disprove that.

Unfortunately, this all gets pretty complicated pretty quickly. If you want to find out more about statistical testing, or have a go at them yourself, most spreadsheet software has the ability to conduct some basic tests. Why not start off by looking at a t-Test (1 and 2 sample) or an Anova (Single and Two-Factor). As mentioned above, these tests often only work if data is normally distributed (if it's not, you may need to convert the data to be normal).

That's it for our statistics introduction – I hope it's provided you with a good overview of key terminology and allows you to understand more of any statistics conversations you might be a part of!

Project Management

Throughout the book you will no doubt have noticed the emphasis placed on projects of business improvement. The fields of project management and business improvement are inextricably linked. Generally speaking, in business improvement there are two kinds of projects: .

- Business improvement initiatives – large scale business-wide (or perhaps function or area-wide) change programmes, such as undertaking the full Understand, Identify, Improve methodology (page 39) across an entire company. We might call this a programme – a programme is a large-scale project, often made up of many smaller projects (or *packages of work*).
- Problem Solving projects – smaller scale projects, ranging in relative size, to solve particular problems or make specific improvements. These can either be identified through BAU (Business As Usual) or via a business improvement initiative.

So, given the importance of projects in the field of business improvement, I wanted to include an overview of the field of project management.

Firstly, there are several things that a project needs in order to be managed properly:

1. Business Justification – there needs to be a clear reason to do an improvement project. What will the project do and will it deliver a benefit to the company?

If a project won't deliver a benefit to the organisation, then it should not proceed. A senior manager or project sponsor will normally sign off on a project before it begins.

2. Managing customers' expectations - thinking about what the customer of your project wants from you and your team. Meeting those expectations but not allowing the customer to demand too much from you by changing the scope of the project (see the final point in this list!).

3. Managing people - running a team of people on a project, or influencing people who you do not directly manage or work with. Project management requires "defined roles and responsibilities" for everyone working on a project, while business improvement is clear in its need for stakeholder and customers to be identified and utilised.

4. Planning - organising the different elements of the project. What needs to be done and when? Typically, projects are broken down into stages. The more you can break it down, then the more manageable it can be. Understanding the critical path of a project is really important here (see page 135). Often, Gantt charts are used for planning projects.

5. Managing risks and issues - understanding what could prevent the project from being completed, and resolving these concerns. A risk is something that might happen whereas an issue is something that has actually occurred. Risks are certainly key in business improvement too.

6. Leading and facilitating - general leadership of the programme of work whilst also running meetings or sessions and capturing as many ideas as necessary to succeed. All of this is done throughout the lifetime of a project.

7. Managing scope – this is particularly important for business improvement projects. Chances are, if you're solving one problem, managers and colleagues will want their own issues and problems solving too! So the thing to avoid here is "Scope creep". As part of the initial planning of a project, you need to clearly state what is *in* or *out* of scope (page 133).

Project Charter

The Project Charter is one of the four key documents needed for a successful project (alongside the project plan (page 135), action tracker (page 144) and a risk register (page 145). The charter should be created at the outset of a project and signed off before the project can begin.

Before we go any further, I just want to be clear – you do not need a project charter (or indeed all the formal project documents) for every small project that you do. If a problem can be solved via a 7-Step one-pager then that should cover all your needs here. The key is to use the documents that are proportionate to your needs – use your discretion.

A project charter is a simplified, smaller scale version of a business case for a particular project or initiative. It explains *why* a particular activity should be done. Project charters are ideal for most improvement or problem solving projects. If there's a much bigger investment or a larger project, a business case will likely need to be developed instead (it contains all the same information as a project charter, but in a larger, report format, with all background calculations and appendices included).

As discussed, a project charter is presented at the beginning of a project. It needs to be agreed to and signed off by the project sponsor and any other key stakeholders (e.g. if there's a large cost implication then finance may need to sign it, or if people are being seconded for an extended period of time, their line managers will need to agree). It's best to get the approval of anyone involved to sign the project charter – in doing so they are agreeing to the scope of the project (thereby reducing the risk of scope creep!) and are agreeing that there is a clear benefit and business need for it to take place.

I've added a project charter template to the appendices, you can find this on page 158. For now, we'll go through each of the elements of a good project charter.

<u>Heading Section</u>

For the heading section, we'll add all the core information required at the outset of a project:

- Project title – the name of the project (e.g. the name of the problem we're solving)
- Project leader – the person leading the project
- Start and end date – date started and the approximate (expected) end date – based on the project plan
- Location – establishing exactly where the project is being undertaken can help reinforce the project scope which we outline further on in the charter
- Project sponsor – a senior manager who agrees to sponsor the project

Project Title:		Project Lead/Manager:	
Start Date:		Approx. End Date:	
Location/ Area:		Project Sponsor:	

<u>Overall Summary</u>

Now we provide additional context for the project. For an executive summary we need to answer the question: What does this project aim to achieve? For problem solving projects we also add the problem and goal statements here.

Project Executive Summary:			
[Summary of the project in a paragraph or two.]			
Proble m Statem ent:		Goal State ment:	

Project Scope

All projects need a clear definition of where its boundaries lie. I find it best to simply provide two lists; in scope and out of scope. As an example, I've filled in the below table for our problem statement used earlier on:

- From June 2021 to June 2022, 8% of Product A failed at visual inspection after machining. This led to a rework process costing £200 per component (£240,000 in total)

In Scope:	Product A Process lines 1 and 2 Products failing at visual inspection	Out of Scope :	Products B, C and D All other process lines Products failing at other points

The in and out of scope statements normally mirror each other and do not need to be too overcomplicated. This just sets a baseline that everyone agrees to at the outset.

Cost / Benefit Analysis

As part of our justification of this project, we need to show how it will benefit the business. In almost all cases this is via financial benefits. At this stage, when starting a project, it's impossible to know *exactly* how much the project might expect to save. With most improvement projects where we know the area involved, we might look at lost sales (see production or sales constrained on page 70). If we're really struggling a good idea is to break it down in the constituent areas where savings can be made and take an average of the teams estimates of savings.

We also need to outline the other "side of the ledger" – by summarising what the project will cost the business to complete. For example, taking an employee (or a team) out of the day job for a period of time will cost the business money – this needs to be agreed as part of the charter. Note that most businesses have an agreed hourly employee cost (higher than an hourly salary) that should be used to calculate this labour cost for the project.

Once we've understood the benefits and costs, we can work out the payback time for the project. I normally show this in months (for example if the benefits are £100,000/year and the costs are £50,000, the payback time is 6 months). Often, businesses will have a rule where projects need to have a payback time of less than, say, 18 months.

Expected Project Benefits	Expected Project Costs/Budget
Project Payback Time (Months):	

Project Planning

The project plan shown in the Project Charter is not a full project plan (normally I would use a Gantt chart for this). In this document we can add the key milestones (or *stages*, if you prefer) of the project and when they are expected to be completed. Often, depending on the size of the project, this can be advised by a Gantt chart completed in the background with the team, to understand what might be reasonable dates at which to complete certain milestones.

Key Milestones		
	Title	Planned Date
1	*[Milestone Name]*	*[Estimate of completion]*
2		
3		
4		
5		
6		

Project Team, Stakeholders and Comms Plan

Understanding who can help and who needs to be kept informed during a project is also very important at the outset. Think about all the skills and knowledge you'll need and ensure this is reflected in the project team. We'll list team members names and job titles here:

Project Team
[Names and job titles of all team members]

We'll list the names and job titles of the other stakeholders below, before completing a simple stakeholder analysis to understand what our communications plan should be. See below:

Other Stakeholders	Comms Planning
[Names and job titles of all stakeholders]	*[Planned approach for each of:* *Keep Satisfied, Manage Closely,* *Monitor and Keep Informed]*

Stakeholders are assessed in a similar way to projects in an ease / effect matrix (page 83). We can list our stakeholders in a table before giving them a score (normally out of 10) against influence (the power they have over the project area) and interest (how much interest they have in the project).

Once the stakeholders are assessed, we can plot them on a graph as below:

Stakeholder Analysis

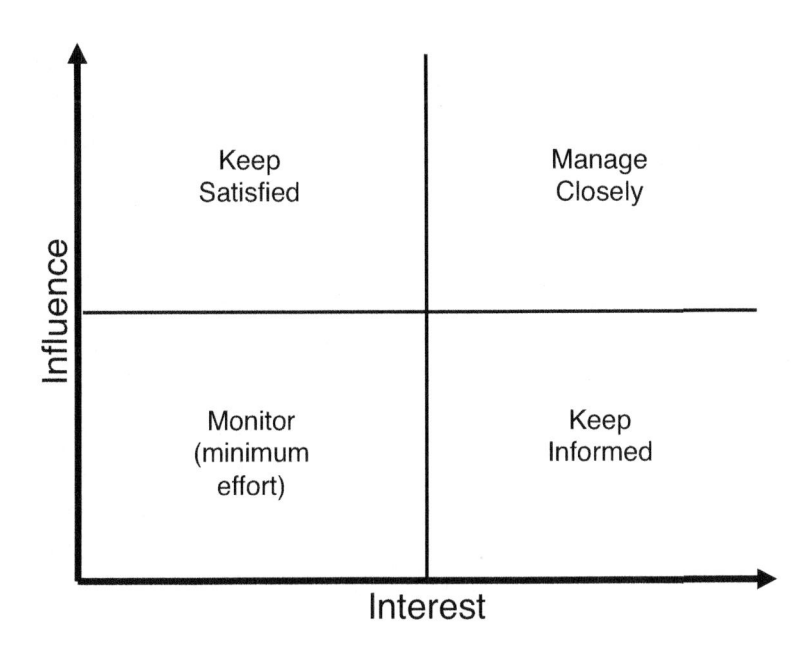

Our comms plan is now advised by which of the four quadrants the stakeholders fit into. It's down to a project managers discretion but, for example, you might choose to just do a weekly email for those with limited influence (Monitor and Keep Informed), whilst regular meetings could take place with those in the Manage Closely category. It's a good idea to make sure all identified stakeholders are fully aware of the Project Charter contents and have their own copy.

Weekly emails or other updates might include sections of our project charter – for example highlighting key risks or milestones that have been achieved. All of this comes under the banner of "project governance" – key to any successful project.

Project Risks

A project risk register is a living document (meaning it is regularly updated throughout a project). However, within the charter, we highlight the key risks identified at the outset (we'll cover risk management further on page 145).

Project Risks

Approval and Sign-Off

Finally, to complete the project charter, we need approval from the project's senior stakeholders. By signing and dating they agree to all the elements of the project charter – allowing the project to begin in earnest.

Project Approval:		
Name	Signature	Date

Remember you can see the full project charter template in the appendices (page 158).

Project Planning

For smaller projects, a simple list of milestones and when they need to be achieved can be enough. However, sometimes a more robust project plan is needed. For this, a Gantt chart is often the best option.

Completing the project plan as a team can help you understand the different workstreams and stages involved, as well as where dependencies lie and, crucially, the critical path. In my other book, Business English Quick, I outlined an example of making a simple meal to summarise what we mean by critical path. Using a similar example, we'll now explore Gantt chart layouts and the critical path in more detail.

First off, here's all the steps we need to complete for our simple meal:

- Chop tomatoes (2 minutes)
- Chop herbs (1 minute)
- Boil water (2 minutes)
- Cook pasta (10 minutes)
- Drain [empty out] pasta (30 seconds)
- Cook tomato sauce (5 minutes)
- Mix pasta and sauce (1 minute)

Now, we'll plan this by putting it into a Gantt chart. This allows us to display activities along a time scale (with the position and length of the bar indicating its order and duration). We used a simple Gantt chart earlier when looking at SMED exercises (page 107). Our first iteration of the Gantt chart might look like the following:

Gantt Chart Planning Example: First Iteration

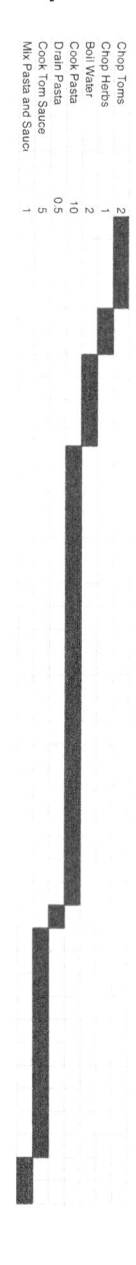

Now, as a team we have a baseline to work from, and can review each of these activities to understand which of them are dependent on one another and which can be done in unison. After working through this, our Gantt chart will look more like the following:

Gantt Chart Planning Example: Second Iteration

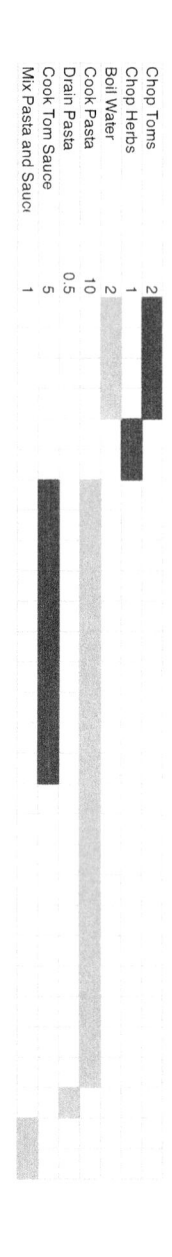

Now we've identified two paths through this particular project. Our critical path (that needs to be prioritised) is that of boiling water and cooking pasta, most of which can be done at the same time as preparation of the tomato sauce. This has saved us 8 minutes of total time!

Of course, this is a simple example and may seem obvious, but if we apply the same principles to a larger scale project – the time savings can be huge. Planning properly is a crucial skill in efficient and effective project management. Remember the saying; failure to plan means planning to fail!

Action Tracking

Sometimes tasks that need to be completed as part of a project are too small to be included on a Gantt chart, but certainly too big to ignore. To manage these actions, it's a good idea to create a simple action tracker. When I'm managing projects, I like to run through these actions during regular meetings (e.g. weekly). The whole team can then have visibility of who has done what and have some level of accountability for the actions they needed to do. Action trackers do not need to be complicated, something like the below will suffice:

Action Tracking Table Example

#	Action	Name	Date Planned	Status (RAG)
1	*[Name of action]*	*[Person completing]*	*[Expected completion date]*	*[Red, Amber or Green depending on status]*
2				

As long as this is regularly reviewed, alongside a wider look at the project plan and milestone achievement, the projects current state can be quickly understood by all involved.

Risk Management

An important but all too often overlooked area of project management is risk management. A key document that every project should have is a risk register (we can of course draw the line at smaller projects that are part of the day job – but some thought should still be given to risks, even if it isn't formally recorded).

Holistically, when considering risk at a business level, a Lean organisation manages a delicate balance between business improvement and risk management. Business improvement can sometimes get a bad reputation where this equilibrium is not considered. Companies should not "cut to the bone" on labour, for example, misunderstanding that whilst in the short-term costs can be saved, in the long-term vital skills and capabilities may have been lost forever. A good business improver always thinks about maintaining the ability to meet what the customer wants – as per our elements of Lean discussed at the outset (page 21).

Anyway, back to considering risk at a project level and the creation of our risk register. You can see a risk register template in appendix V (page 162). The first step is to sit down as a team and brainstorm all the potential risks (things that could go wrong) as part of a project. Here's some examples of typical risks commonly considered in projects:

- Team members have other priorities that they need to focus on
- Scope creep
- Contractor / supplier delays
- Planning or estimation errors
- Natural disasters
- Time pressures on project

Once the risks have been identified, they require recording as part of the risk register document against the following areas:

- Date risk raised
- Description – title and description of the risk
- Likelihood – score out of 10 for how likely a risk is to materialise
- Impact – score out of 10 for how big an impact the risk would have on a project
- Severity – multiplication of likelihood and impact, giving an overall risk score
- Risk Owner – person responsible for managing and mitigating a given risk
- Actions – actions required to mitigate (or reduce the risk)
- Deadline – when those actions are required/expected to be completed

The final two areas (actions and deadline) might only be completed after all the initial risks are recorded. With those scoring highest on severity requiring mitigation most urgently. As an example, if poor communication during the project is a risk, a clear communication plan can be developed and adhered to in order to reduce that risk.

As part of a larger project, the risk register should be reviewed on a regular basis (perhaps weekly or fortnightly) – this ensures that effective risk management is in place for the duration of the project. Any individual actions may also be recorded on the project action tracker – where further risk identification or mitigation is required during the project.

As a final word on risk management – remember that if a risk materialises then it can be considered a problem to be resolved using one or more of the techniques discussed earlier in this book. Usually the 7-Step approach (page 102) will be able to resolve most issues.

Waterfall or Agile

Just like business improvement, project management has its own methodologies or ways of working. Two of the most often mentioned are Waterfall and Agile.

In waterfall project management, a project is split into manageable chunks, each with their own deliverable. This methodology is sometimes instead referred to as "management by stages". Normally, each time a project reaches the end of a stage (or milestone), senior stakeholders are involved in approving the projects movement to the next one. The gold standard for this kind of structured project management is PRINCE2 (PRINCE meaning Projects in a Controlled Environment), this methodology was originally created by the UK government but is now also used in many private sector projects and programme management internationally.

Agile is a newer approach originating in project management for software development. It deserves a mention in a business improvement book, however, because of its focus on customer feedback and requirements often resulting in lower costs and speedier delivery. An agile project is broken down even further and up-front planning is kept to a minimum in order to get the project moving – it's all about delivering value as soon as possible. At the end of iterations (effectively attempts at solutions), progress is reviewed and customer requirements re-visited to ensure the project is moving at pace and in the right direction.

Both of these approaches have merit and have been used successfully across many different industries. Often the best approach, particularly with larger projects, is to try to take the best of both worlds. Large-scale initiatives usually require the rigour of a waterfall methodology, whilst smaller stages within that project could have the freedom to be managed in a more agile manner. If you'd like to learn more about these two approaches to project management (and indeed, other approaches) I recommend searching online.

<u>Summary and</u>

<u>Conclusion</u>

Fundamentally, businesses exist in order to make money. This is often measured most effectively in terms of profit. Particularly in a sales constrained environment, there are two ways to impact this bottom line:

1. Increase the price of the product(s)

   Product pricing is often market driven, meaning it's difficult to increase without a reduction in either sales or customer satisfaction.

2. Do or make the product(s) at lower cost

   Now you've read this book you should know how to take this approach. Business Improvement is all about doing more with less – finding the most efficient way possible.

I hope it's clear to you now just how powerful a tool business improvement can be for positive change in any organisation.

If you're just starting out in business improvement, don't expect to become an expert overnight. Business improvement is a continual cycle of learning and applying best practise – much like self-improvement. Remember to adopt the Understand, Identify, Improve process in your career and in your organisation;

1. Understand – first understand the scenario you find yourself in
2. Identify – hone in on specific areas of interest to discover what might be improved
3. Improve – undertake the identified improvements to change the organisation for the better

Improvement is all about breaking a problem down into manageable chunks – clever use of business improvement and project management skills can allow for proper, permanent resolution of issues and, crucially, cost savings across an organisation.

Many of the tools and techniques outlined in this book can be put into practice immediately – why not think of how you might apply them right now to make a difference in your role?

You can download all the templates (which are also in the appendices over the following pages) to help you get started.

www.BusinessImprovementQuick.com

Thank you for reading this book – I hope you've found it useful.

Appendix I – Go-Look-See Template

Templates are available to download at:

www.BusinessImprovementQuick.com/downloads

Go-Look-See Location:	
Date/Time:	
Name:	

Waste Observations:

	Example(s)	Cause(s)
Transportation		
Inventory		
Motion		
Waiting		
Overproduction		
Overprocessing		
Defects		

Other/Unknown		

(Approximate) Process Map*:

Highlight numbers of operators, cleanliness, whether machines were idle or working and any other key observations on your map above.

SWOT Summary:

Strengths:	Weaknesses:
Opportunities:	Threats:

Appendix II – PFMEA Template

Templates are available to download at:

www.BusinessImprovementQuick.com/downloads

Process Step	Potential Failure Mode	Potential Failure Effect(s)	Current Monitoring / Controls	Severity	Likelihood	Detectability	Risk Score	Actions Required	Responsible (Name)	Date Required	Actions Taken	New Severity	New Likelihood	New Detectability	New Risk Score	Comments

Process / Product:

Owner:

Completed by (names):

Date Created:

Date last updated:

Appendix III – Project Charter Template

Templates are available to download at:

www.BusinessImprovementQuick.com/downloads

Project Title:		Project Lead/Manager:	
Start Date:		Approx. End Date:	
Location/Area:		Project Sponsor:	

Project Executive Summary:

| Problem Statement: | | Goal Statement: | |
| In Scope | | Not In Scope | |

Expected Project Benefits	Expected Project Costs/Budget

Project Payback Time (Months):

Key Milestones	Project Team

	Title	Planned Date		
1				
2				
3				
4				
5				
6				

Other Stakeholders	Comms Planning

Project Key Risks:	Project Approval:

Name	Signature	Date	

Appendix IV – 7-Step Template

Templates are available to download at:

www.BusinessImprovementQuick.com/downloads

Problem Title:		Owner:	
Date:		Contact:	
Location/Area:			

1. Define the Problem:

4. Identify Root Cause (5Y):

Direct Cause	Direct Cause	Direct Cause	Direct Cause
Why	Why	Why	Why
Why	Why	Why	Why
Why	Why	Why	Why
Why	Why	Why	Why
Why	Why	Why	Why

Root Cause(s):

5. SCAMPER - Improvement Brainstorming:

Substitute	Put to…
Combine	Eliminate
Adapt	Reverse
Modify	

2. Show the Problem:

6. Implement Corrective Actions:

No.	Corrective Action	Resp.	When	RAG

7. Validate Resolution

3. Identify Root Cause (Ishikawa):

Appendix V – Project Risk Register Template

Templates are available to download at:

www.BusinessImprovementQuick.com/downloads

ID #	Date Raised	Description	Likelihood (/10)	Impact (/10)	Severity (Risk Score)	Risk Owner	Mitigating Action(s)	Deadline	Comments
1									
2									
3									

Index

Also by Joseph Mann:

Business English Quick

Business English Quick

- Cheaper than an online English class
- Easy to read and understand
- Learn key foundation content common to many MBA programmes and business courses globally
- Quick vocabulary learning: Includes a glossary of over 350 key business phrases and words – with examples
- Understand Project Management, Finance, Software and much more!

With Business English, communication and context are key to success. This book will give you both. In addition to the core book content, a fully detailed glossary will explain and summarise all the key vocabulary from every section.

Whether you're applying for a new job, have a big presentation coming up or just want to learn some new vocabulary before your next meeting – this book can help.

Topics covered in this book include: Professional English; International English; Types of Business; Business Structures; Finance; Procurement; Marketing; Software; Communication and Correspondence; Applying for Jobs; Interviews and Recruitment; Meetings; Presentations; Project Management; Business Improvement.

www.businessenglishquick.com

About the Author

Joseph Mann is a Business Improvement professional based in the United Kingdom. He graduated from the University of Warwick with a Master's degree in Engineering Business Management following research into Lean culture and improvement. Joseph has travelled extensively; saving companies £m's, coaching business techniques and learning languages. Business Improvement Quick shares insights from both academic research and business experience to help others drive long-lasting improvement in their own organisations.

Printed in Great Britain
by Amazon

18428630R00098